T0090583

THE PSYCHOLOGY OF TIME

What is the meaning of time? Do we have an internal clock? Can time speed up or slow down?

The Psychology of Time considers how we define, describe, and experience time. From a discussion of how our language around time is dependent on metaphor, to the role of biology in controlling our bodily experience of time, the book delves into how the finitude of life is a given human experience. It looks at how we reflect on the passage of time throughout our lives, and how our experience of time can be influenced by diverse factors including our age, gender, health, and culture.

Offering insights into something we are all immersed in, but often give little thought to, *The Psychology of Time* shows us how our understanding and experience of time can influence our everyday behaviour.

Richard Gross has been publishing psychology texts for more than 30 years, including undergraduate textbooks.

THE PSYCHOLOGY OF EVERYTHING

People are fascinated by psychology, and what makes humans tick. Why do we think and behave the way we do? We've all met armchair psychologists claiming to have the answers, and people that ask if psychologists can tell what they're thinking. The Psychology of Everything is a series of books which debunk the popular myths and pseudo-science surrounding some of life's biggest questions.

The series explores the hidden psychological factors that drive us, from our subconscious desires and aversions, to our natural social instincts. Absorbing, informative, and always intriguing, each book is written by an expert in the field, examining how research-based knowledge compares with popular wisdom, and showing how psychology can truly enrich our understanding of modern life.

Applying a psychological lens to an array of topics and contemporary concerns – from sex, to fashion, to conspiracy theories – The Psychology of Everything will make you look at everything in a new way.

Titles in the series:

The Psychology of Belonging
by Kelly-Ann Allen

The Psychology of Art
by George Mather

The Psychology of Wellness
by Gary W. Wood

The Psychology of Comedy
by G Neil Martin

The Psychology of Democracy
by Darren G. Lilleker and Billur Aslan Ozgul

The Psychology of Counselling
by Marie Percival

The Psychology of Travel
by Andrew Stevenson

The Psychology of Attachment
by Robbie Duschinsky, Pehr Granqvist and Tommie Forslund

The Psychology of Running
by Noel Brick and Stuart Holliday

The Psychology of the Teenage Brain
by John Coleman

The Psychology of Time
by Richard Gross

For more information about this series, please visit: www.routledgetextbooks. com/textbooks/thepsychologyofeverything/

THE PSYCHOLOGY
OF TIME

RICHARD GROSS

Routledge
Taylor & Francis Group

LONDON AND NEW YORK

Designed cover image: © Getty Images

First published 2024
by Routledge
4 Park Square, Milton Park, Abingdon, Oxon OX14 4RN

and by Routledge
605 Third Avenue, New York, NY 10158

Routledge is an imprint of the Taylor & Francis Group, an informa business

British Library Cataloguing-in-Publication Data
A catalogue record for this book is available from the British Library

Library of Congress Cataloguing-in-Publication Data
Names: Gross, Richard D., author.
Title: The psychology of time / Richard Gross.
Description: Abingdon, Oxon ; New York, NY : Routledge, 2024. |
Series: The psychology of everything | Includes bibliographical references.
Identifiers: LCCN 2023042062 (print) | LCCN 2023042063 (ebook)
| ISBN 9781032696201 (hardback) | ISBN 9781032696195
(paperback) | ISBN 9781032696218 (ebook)
Subjects: LCSH: Time perception. | Time--Psychological aspects.
Classification: LCC BF468 .G76 2024 (print) | LCC BF468 (ebook) |
DDC 153.7/53--dc23/eng/20231218
LC record available at https://lccn.loc.gov/2023042062
LC ebook record available at https://lccn.loc.gov/2023042063

ISBN: 978-1-032-69620-1 (hbk)
ISBN: 978-1-032-69619-5 (pbk)
ISBN: 978-1-032-69621-8 (ebk)

DOI: 10.4324/9781032696218

Typeset in Joanna
by MPS Limited, Dehradun

CONTENTS

ABOUT THE AUTHOR

I retired from teaching (in Further/Higher Education) in 2000 in order to concentrate on my writing (first publication 1987: *The Science of Mind & Behaviour*, currently in its 8th edition (2020)). I have written a number of Psychology texts for both Hodder Education and Routledge, the latter including *The Psychology of Grief* (in the Psychology of Everything series) and *Understanding Grief: An Introduction*, both based on my work with Cruse Bereavement Support (formerly 'Care') (since 2006).

1

WHAT IS TIME?

TIME AND CONSCIOUSNESS

Time – and its relationship to consciousness (or the role it plays in consciousness) – represents one of the first topics to be discussed in the then-new scientific discipline of Psychology. This is best represented by the classic *Principles of Psychology* (1890) by one of the pioneers of the discipline, the American Psychologist and philosopher, William James.

The importance of time was a dominant theme in James's writings: a major task for Psychology is to account for *change*, over time, in our thoughts and feelings. He claimed that 'thought goes on' in terms of the following five principles:

1. Every thought tends to be part of a personal consciousness.
2. Within each personal consciousness, thought is always changing.
3. Within each personal consciousness, thought is sensibly continuous.
4. It always appears to deal with objects other than itself.
5. It is interested in some parts of these objects to the exclusion of others, and welcomes or rejects – *chooses* from them, in a word – all the while.[1]

DOI: 10.4324/9781032696218-1

The claim that 'thought is always changing' is elaborated in the following;

> ... no state once gone can recur and be identical with what it was before ...[2]
>
> ... there is no proof that the same bodily sensation is ever got by us twice. What is got twice is the same OBJECT ... The sameness of *things* is what we are concerned to ascertain; and any sensations that assure us of that will probably be considered in a rough way to be the same with each other.[3]
>
> Experience is remoulding us every moment, and our mental reaction on every given thing is really a resultant of our experience of the whole world up to that date.[4]

James proceeds to argue that 'thought feels continuous', so that:

> ... even where there is a time-gap, the consciousness after it feels as if it belonged together with the consciousness before it, as another part of the same self; and likewise... changes ... in the quality of consciousness are never absolutely abrupt. (p. 237)[5]

James slides seamlessly from talking about the continuity we attribute to *objects* – despite changes in our sensations – to the claim regarding the continuity of *consciousness* or *self*.[6] The feeling of continuity in our *experience of objects* is, by implication, what gives consciousness its 'stream-like' quality, and hence the feeling of self-identity.

The 'stream of thought' is, of course, a *metaphor* and we shall discuss in Chapter 2 the extent to which time-related metaphors are commonly found in English. For James, the contents of human consciousness are better likened to a stream than a collection of discrete elements or ideas. The Greek philosopher, Heraclitus, famously observed that one can never step into the same stream twice: while the river banks and the course remain essentially the same, the water is constantly changing. By analogy, we can never have the identical sensation, idea or other experience twice (see the first two quotes above).

Similarly, a stream and consciousness both display *continuousness* (or continuity) (see third quote above).

> Even when gaps occur in consciousness, as in anaesthesia, epileptic seizures, or sleep, a subjective sense of continuity is maintained. The remembered experiences immediately before and after the periods of consciousness – 'the broken edges of sentient life', as James put it – seem to 'meet and merge over the gap, much as the feelings of space of the opposite margins of the 'blind spot' meet and merge over the objective interruption to the sensitiveness of the eye. Such consciousness as this, whatever it be for the onlooking psychologist, is for itself unbroken. It feels unbroken' (James, 1890, pp. 237–8).[7]

In much the same way, our constant, regular, usually unconscious blinking doesn't result in a series of unrelated views of the external world: the brain 'fills in' these brief time gaps in order to produce a continuous, subjectively uninterrupted view.

Our consciousness 'unrolls in time'.[8] We can imagine abolishing space from our awareness (say, through floating in a sensory deprivation tank) but it's almost impossible to imagine abolishing *time* from one's awareness. The fact that there are no known cultures without some intuitive conception of time suggests that this is an inherent feature of human nature (albeit shaped by cultural and historical factors).

> I stop and do nothing. Nothing happens. I am thinking about nothing. I listen to the passing of time.

> This is time, familiar and intimate ... The rush of seconds, hours, years that hurls us towards life then drags us towards nothingness ... We inhabit time as fish live in water. Our being

is being in time ... the universe unfolds into the future, dragged by time, and exists according to the order of time.[9]

As Rovelli, the much-admired Italian theoretical physicist, says, we're so immersed in, and surrounded by, time, that we're often unaware of it (just as fish are the last to 'discover' water). Consistent with James's stream of consciousness, Rovelli goes on to say that, universally, time is seen as *flowing*; this probably seems in many ways *obvious*.

As you read this sentence, you probably think that this moment – right now – is what is happening. The present moment feels special. It is real. However much you may remember the past or anticipate the future, you live in the present. Of course, the moment during which you read that sentence is no longer happening. This one is ...[10]

In other words, it feels as though time flows: the present is constantly updating itself. '... We have a deep intuition that the future is open until it becomes present and that the past is fixed. As time flows, this structure of fixed past, immediate present and open future gets carried forward in time ...'[11] This structure is built into our language (see Chapter 2), thought (see Chapter 4) and behaviour (see Chapter 5).

As natural as this way of thinking is, however, it's not what physicists understand by time. The equations of physics don't tell us which events are occurring *right now* – they're like a map without the 'you are here' symbol. The present moment doesn't exist in these equations, so neither does the flow of time. According to Albert Einstein's theories of *relativity*, not only is there no single special present, but all moments are equally real: fundamentally, the future is no more 'open' than the past.

The gap between the scientific and our everyday understanding of time has troubled thinkers throughout history and has widened as physicists have gradually stripped time of most of the characteristics we commonly attribute to it.

> ... the time of physics and the time of experience is reaching its logical conclusion, for many in theoretical physics have come to believe that time fundamentally does not even exist.[12]

But how could this be? Everything we do, we do in time: so much of what we do, individually and collectively (as a society) is governed by time – at least, time as measured by clocks and other equivalent devices.

TIME, CONSCIOUSNESS, AND FREE WILL

The issue of free will has, in various guises, been central to Western philosophy since the Ancient Greeks. Kant (1787/1996), Sartre (1943/1956), Heidegger (1927/1962), Merleau-Ponty (1964), and Fromm (1941) all debated the existence and importance of free will. For Sartre, freedom is *absolute* and defines what being human means; Merleau-Ponty also saw freedom as central to human existence – but it's *not* absolute.

Libet, a French neuroscientist, is best known for his study of the *temporal relations* between neural (brain) events and experience, specifically, his finding that we unconsciously decide to act well *before* we think we've made the decision to act. This, of course, has major implications for the notion of free will: commonsense, at least, would say that our *conscious* decision to act is what constitutes free will and this *precedes* the action.

Libet's findings suggest that being conscious of having made a decision might be best thought of as a *result* of brain processes that actually do the work, rather than as part of the causal chain of events leading up to a decision. While this provides evidence for those who argue *against* the existence of free will, Libet pointed out that even if the movement were initiated by unconscious forces, there's still ample time to *veto* the act, once we're aware of our intentions; in other words, there's time for us to change our minds, which is consistent with the commonsense view of free will. (Libet's research is discussed in detail in Chapter 4.)

NEWTON'S AND EINSTEIN'S TIME

If 'clock time' is merely a convenient way of regulating and coordinating our behaviour, we still want to know what it is that clocks etc. are actually measuring.

In *Principia Mathematica* (1687), Newton describes the laws of motion and universal gravitation; this represented the scientific foundation of classical mechanics which dominated physics for the next 220 years or so. For Newton, *absolute time* exists as a constant force in the universe; it is mathematically true and is different from *apparent time* (based on the careful measurement of motions, which are essentially *spatial* – not *temporal*). This distinction is fundamental and continues to echo current debates regarding the nature of time in relation to space.[13]

> *Absolute*, true, and mathematical time, in and of itself and of its own nature, without reference to anything external, *flows uniformly* and by another name is called duration. *Relative*, apparent, and common time is any sensible measure ... of duration by means of motion: such a measure – for example, an hour, a day, a month, a year – is commonly used instead of true time.[14]

The world is equipped with a 'master clock', which uniquely and objectively carves the world up into instants of time.

> In astronomy, absolute time is distinguished from relative time by the equation of common time. For natural days, which are commonly considered equal for the purposes of measuring time, are usually unequal. Astronomers correct this inequality in

order to measure celestial motions on the basis of a truer time ... the *flow of absolute time* cannot be changed.[15]

So, critical aspects of Newton's view of time for the psychology of time are (i) the distinction between absolute and relative time; (ii) the flow of absolute time; and (iii) the equation between this flow and 'duration'.

Superimposed onto the 'flow' of time (or perhaps more accurately, drawn 'through' the flow) is the idea of the 'arrow of time'; this tells us which direction is the future: past→present→future is the only way that time can run. 'Time' (the master clock) brings the concepts of order, continuity, duration, simultaneity, flow, and the arrow together;[16] this is reflected to a large extent in our commonsense understanding of 'time'. We just accept, unquestioningly, that time exists in some objective way and is what is measured – more or less accurately – by 'timepieces'.

So, beginning with Newton, we understood time as '... something that flows uniformly and equally throughout the universe, in the course of which all things happen ...'.[17] There exists a 'now', throughout the cosmos, and this 'now' constitutes reality. The arrow of time is also part of that reality.

However, this familiar picture has 'fallen apart' and is only an 'approximation of a much more complex reality'.[18]

> A present that is common throughout the whole universe does not exist ... Events are not ordered in pasts, presents and futures; they are only 'partially' ordered. There is a present that is near to us, but nothing that is 'present' in a far-off galaxy. The present is a *localized* rather than a *global* phenomenon.[19]

Einstein's (1905) *special theory of relativity* (STR) dispensed with the idea of absolute simultaneity: what events are happening at the same time depends on how fast you're going. The true arena of events isn't time or space, but their union: *spacetime*. Two observers moving at different speeds will disagree about when and where an event occurs – but they will agree about its spacetime location. Then in 1916, Einstein's *general theory of relativity* (GTR) extended the STR to situations that involve the operation of gravity: this distorts time, such that the passage of a second 'here' may not mean the same as the passage of a second 'there'. So, we cannot generally think about the world as unfolding, tick by tick, according to a single time parameter.[20]

Physicists understand, say, a table, as a swarm of particles comprising mostly empty space; this couldn't be much more different from our immediate perceptual experience of a solid, three-dimensional object. These two 'realities' don't usually compete with each other in the 'truth stakes', but according to *reductionists*, the physicist's version represents the 'ultimate' truth'.

Although time may not exist at a fundamental level (equivalent to the physicist's particles), it may arise at higher levels (equivalent to the solid 3-D table of everyday experience). From the swarm of particles, solidity may emerge (hence, an *emergent property* of the particles): time too could be an emergent property of whatever the basic ingredients of the world are.

CLOCKS AND THE EXPERIENCE OF TIME

> At the most fundamental level that we currently know of … there is little that resembles time as we experience it. There is no special variable 'time', there is no difference between past and future …[21]

As important as it is to see how theoretical physics makes sense of time, most of us aren't theoretical physicists; even if we were, this wouldn't impact our everyday experience of time. Clearly, we do 'carve up' time into smaller or larger 'portions': 'past' ('last century', 'last week', 'yesterday', 'ten minutes ago', 'just now'), 'present' ('now'), and 'future' (next century', next week', 'in ten minutes'). Our language (the English language, at least) reflects the extent of our 'immersion' in time (see Chapter 2).

Commonsense, everyday understanding of time is governed hugely by the way we measure it. If clocks measure anything, then surely, it's time: we think of time as comparable to other things that we (can) measure, such as weight, height, distance, and speed. While the first two denote properties of tangible objects (or people and other animals), the second two are less 'graspable', more 'abstract', not so much properties of things but more the product of taking certain kinds of measurements or recording events.

In terms of this distinction, time is much more like distance and speed than weight and height. But because clocks etc. are such a familiar feature of everyday life and specified times regulate so much individual and social behaviour, it feels *as if* time is 'graspable' and accessible. Also, because we *divide* time up into units – seconds, minutes, hours etc. – we think of it as discrete or discontinuous: it must be *divisible* because we can measure it.

> I say, e.g. that a minute has just elapsed, and I mean by this that a pendulum, beating the seconds, has completed sixty oscillations. If I picture these sixty oscillations to myself … I do not think of sixty strokes which succeed one another, but of sixty points on a fixed line, each one of which symbolizes … an oscillation.[22]

According to the French philosopher, Henri Bergson, real time *cannot* be divisible; rather, it's a continuous and unmeasurable *duration* of the past flowing into the present. In real time, there's 'pure duration'; time in immediate experience isn't broken into parts but is a continuous stream. So, according to Bergson, clocks and other timepieces mislead us into thinking that time is a real, objective feature of the world that can be measured by breaking it down into units, some smaller, some larger.

We're also misled about the reality of time by confusing it with its *perceptible effects*. Just as 'wind' and gravity' are only known through what they bring about (e.g. the windchimes tinkle without anyone being nearby; the apple falls from the tree onto the ground), so 'time' is something we infer from particular events (typically changes) that we witness (e.g. the 'interval' between switching the kettle on and it's turning itself off when the water has boiled).

In all these cases, we cannot literally perceive what we believe to account for the witnessed events; instead, we are taking those events as evidence of the operation and existence of wind, gravity, or time. While the first two have a theoretical underpinning (such as meteorological accounts of wind in terms of isobars; and Newton's account of gravity), does inferring 'time' from the kettle being switched on and then turning itself off add to our understanding of what's taking place? At best, it may contribute to the description of what's happening, but does it really explain anything?

Maybe not. But experiencing time as speeding up, slowing down, or even coming to a stop, is very real and there's plenty of research which shows these experiences occur quite reliably under particular sets of circumstances (see Chapter 4).

TIME AND DURATION

In its most generic sense, time is defined as 'the system of those sequential relations that any event has to any other, as past, present, or future; indefinite and continuous duration regarded as that in which events succeed one another.' In contrast, duration refers to 'the length of time something continues or exists. ...'[23]

In other words, time refers to the ordinal succession of events from the past to the future; duration refers to the 'relative expand' of a particular individual event. Rochat uses the analogy of numbers: any number has both an ordinal aspect (e.g. '3 is larger than 2 and smaller than 4') and a cardinal aspect ('the "three-ness" of number 3'). So, 'time' is 'ordinal' while 'duration' is cardinal; by definition, order implies/involves a comparison (here, between different events), while 'duration' implies/involves focus on a single, specific event.[24]

The cardinal aspect is subjective (or 'relative'): the 'three-ness' of three will mean different things to different people (or may mean nothing at all!), just as people will differ in how they experience waiting in line for an hour to get into a concert. By contrast, the ordinal aspect is 'absolute': it means the same for everyone because it's a property of the number itself.[25]

Heidegger's 'Dasein'

However, does the necessary ordinal logic of time (it can be defined or measured independently of individuals) make it more *real* than duration? While it exists independently of individual experience, this is, arguably, precisely what makes it *less* real: it's more abstract and removed from *Dasein* ('being there'),[26] our embodied experiential presence in the world. Heidegger, the influential existentialist and phenomenologist, is the first Western philosopher to have attempted to provide an understanding of humans' uniquely self-conscious and introspective experience of 'being', to capture the essence of human subjectivity.

For Heidegger, *Dasein* is defined by our relationship to time, in particular, finite time.

> *Sorge* (concern with doing) guides *Dasein* (my being) as it falls into the world, with always the absolute and inescapable end of this fall in sight ... we act and do as we go about, finite time in mind. In final existential analysis, subjectivity ... is grounded in space (action) and time (finitude and historicity of being).[27]

'Time temporalizes itself only to the extent that it is human'.[28] 'Time is the time of mankind, the time for doing, for that with which mankind is engaged ...';[29] the internal consciousness of time is the horizon of being itself.[30]

> The grounding of the self in time and space is most evident when considering the physicality of the body in the world, as it forms and decays. Our experience of being is trapped within and inseparable from the body which is in constant change until it vanishes. What is unique in human subjective experience is that

we can knowingly (consciously) observe and reflect on such experience as it happens and until it ends. Other creatures feel and perceive their body as they act and move in the world, but presumably without the peculiar human curse of self-consciousness, our poisoned gift from nature, source of all our metaphysical tortures.[31]

A major example of such 'metaphysical tortures' is the recognition that we all die, making us the only species that possesses such knowledge (see *Death* and *time*, Chapter 6).

While our body is the 'vessel' we inhabit from conception to death, this is inseparable from the self-conscious beings that we are: we *are* the vessel. Our body is both an object-for others (in space) and a body-for self; only we, of course, can know what it's like to be (in) our body.

The body I inhabit is also an object *in time* as it moves and acts, driven by the necessary concern of doing something in order to survive, to move, and act on things ... an entity that is spatially unique and temporally finite ...[32]

Perception of duration and judging the passage of time

An important distinction has been made between two main types of perception or judgement about time:

- *Perception of duration* (PoD) refers to our ability to judge how long an interval, stimulus, or event lasted. This is further divided into (i) *prospective* and (ii) *retrospective* judgements: in (i), we know that we'll be required to make a judgement of duration ahead of the event (e.g. 'listen to this music clip; when it's finished, you'll be asked how long it lasted'); in (ii) we don't know in advance that we'll be asked to make a time judgement (e.g. 'How long do you think it took you to read this paragraph?'). (See Chapter 4 for an account of some relevant studies of duration perception.)

- *Passage of time judgements* (PoTJs) refer to judgements of how quickly time seems to pass in any given situation (not a judgement of their duration, although we often express them in that way, as in 'That lecture seemed to go on for hours'). PoTJs are more of a 'feeling' judgement, a *hedonistic* expression of boredom, engagement, or frustration.[33]

Both PoD and PoTJs relate to mind time (again, see Chapter 4).

KANTIAN TIME

Immanuel Kant (1724–1804) was one of the most influential of the 18th-century Enlightenment philosophers, along with John Locke (1632–1704) and David Hume (1711–1776). While Locke and Hume were British *empiricists* (who, especially Locke, had a huge impact on the development of science in general, and Psychology in particular), the German Kant favoured *transcendental idealism*, a blend or synthesis of empiricism and early modern *rationalism*, which, in broad outline, works well in today's nature-nurture debate.[34] The mind isn't a mere associator of sensory impressions (as held by Locke and Hume in Kant's day, and the *connectionism* of the 1980s), nor does it come equipped with actual knowledge about the contents of the world (as in some versions of the rationalism of his day and today's extreme nativism).

> What the innate apparatus of the mind contributes is a set of abstract conceptual frameworks that organize our experience – space, time, substance, causation, number, and logic (today we might add ... living things, other minds, language) ...[35]

Despite the wide differences between empiricism and Kant's form of rationalism, they both focused on how we come to know the world in our minds and through the senses ('empirical' = 'through the senses'), as distinct from God or some other heavenly source. Each of these innate, empty mental forms/categories must be 'filled in' by actual sensory experience or imagining such experience.

Time and space, like causality and number, are *a priori* mental categories (*intuitions* or *immediate representations* of the world). These are different from concepts (which we usually regard as dependent on learning and experience); they are some sort of 'constitutive mental filters', inherent features of the mind, part of 'how the mind works'. This describes Kant's form of *nativism*. While an extreme version would claim that knowledge, abilities etc. are innate or inborn, Kant's view is consistent with Chomsky's (1965) view of language, most forms of Evolutionary Psychology, and the approach in cognitive development called *domain specificity*:[36] the human mind comprises a set of distinct capacities or predispositions which shape/act – and depend – upon sensory experience.

As *a priori* categories of knowledge, time and space would automatically organize the 'raw' sensory experience of the world, giving it immediate meaning and constraining how we make sense of the world.

> Time is not an empirical concept that is somehow drawn from experience. For simultaneity or succession would not them-selves come into perception if the representation of time did not ground them a priori. Only under its presuppositions can one represent that several things exist at one and the same time (simultaneously) or in different times (successively).[37]

Both time and space (as well as number and causality) are, for Kant, evolved products of the human mind, not existing as such in the real (external) world; this means that they cannot be learned through experience, contrary to the claims of Locke and Hume.

> One could say that time, like the categories of space, causality, or numbers are nothing but necessary and helpful illusions of the mind, that we evolved as a species to best reflect and self-reflect, that is, "think" about the ... real world.[38]

Kant also claimed that space is somehow *derived* from time: time has an *ontological precedence* over time. This idea mirrors Newton's view of an absolute time, which reflects the need to account for the duration and perseverance of all things that exist in the constant flow of absolute time.

DIFFERENT KINDS OF TIME

We've already identified three major kinds of time:

1. Time as described and defined by *physicists* can itself take fundamentally different forms: Newton's objective, absolute time in contrast with Einstein's view of the relativity of time.
2. '*Clock time*' is self-explanatory and is often taken implicitly to stand for 'time' in general – unless it's made explicit that some alternative kind is being discussed.
3. The *subjective experience* of time flowing, and the related sense of time as an arrow (a straight line travelling in one direction, from past, through present, to future) is often called '*mind*' (or '*brain*') time. But there's much more to mind time than just these subjective time representations; it can manifest in various ways, including the experience of time speeding up as we get older,[39] the greater accuracy of time estimations the smaller the intervals we're trying to estimate,[40] the speed at which time seems to pass in different situations (such as the slowing-down of time in situations of great stress or danger),[41] and the experience of having been somewhere or done something before when it's in actual fact happening for the first time (*déjà vu*).[42] These – and other examples of distortions of time perception – are discussed in Chapter 4.

As well as different subjective experiences of time, 'mind time' embraces all cases of memory influencing *mental time travel* (MTT),[43] the uniquely human ability to *transcend* time. Language and MTT probably co-evolved (see Chapter 2); in turn, these are both related to memory[44] (see Chapter 4).

4. *Developmental time* refers to the various ways in which we view our lives as divided into 'chunks' of time. Probably the earliest reference in any kind of literature to what a *human life span* (or 'lifetime') comprises appears in the Old Testament:[45] 'The days of our years are three score and ten'. So, traditionally, 70 has been taken as the average duration of a human lifetime. However, until about 200 years ago, people died young and relatively quickly – mainly from infections. *Life expectancy* has been climbing steadily during that period: during the 1900s, average life expectancy in the world doubled, and people in developed countries now tend to die old and slowly – from degenerative diseases brought on by ageing.[46] However, life expectancy cannot just continue rising: based on the analysis of more than a century's worth of data from the UK, the US, and Japan (which boast the largest number of people aged 110 or over), it has been concluded that the maximum human lifespan is fixed at 115.[47] (However, the world's oldest person who ever lived, Jeanne Calment, died in 1997 at the age of 122.).

We often hear (usually older) people predict that such-and-such an event (such as Tottenham Hotspur becoming Premier League Champions) "won't happen in my lifetime". Usually, this 'something' is a much sought-after event or achievement; it's an example of MTT, based on an (implicit) expectation regarding how long the individual is likely to live.

A different form of developmental time refers to how we think of our lifetimes as divisible into separate – but overlapping – stages, such as infancy, childhood, adolescence, adulthood, and old age. Famously, in Shakespeare's *As You like It*, Jacques claims that

All the world's a stage
And all the men and women merely players
They have their exits and their entrances,
And one man in his time plays many parts,
His acts being seven ages ...

The seven ages (or 'stages') are: infancy ('At first the infant, mewling and puking in the nurse's arms'); schoolboy ('... with his satchel ... creeping like a snail unwillingly to school'); teenager ('the lover ...'); young man ('a soldier ... jealous in honour, sudden and quick to quarrel ...'); middle-aged ('the justice ... full of wise saws, and modern instances'); old man ('With spectacles on nose ... his big manly voice turning again towards childish treble pipes and whistles in his sound'); Dotage and death ('Sans teeth, sans eyes, sans taste, sans everything').

Freud identified four stages of psychosexual development (a central part of his psychoanalytic theory). Erik Erikson built on Freud's stages to identity 'The Eight Ages of Man', so going one better than Shakespeare in proposing psychosocial stages.[48] Death and time is discussed in Chapter 6.

If asked to construct a 'time line' (or 'life line'), people typically identify a number of marker events, including (i) achievements and happy events and (ii) setbacks or crises (such as being born, starting school leaving home, starting work, changing jobs or being made redundant, getting married and/or divorced, having children, major bereavements, illnesses, going bankrupt). Clearly, what counts as marker events (or major life changes) varies between cultures, as well as between individuals within a particular culture. Cultural time is discussed in Chapter 5. Marker events are also likely to be defined – and perceived – differently according to gender (again, see Chapter 5).

Developmental time can also refer to how we change our perception of time – in particular, the future – as we progress through the life cycle. According to the theory of the evolution of adult consciousness, alongside the 'shedding' of childhood consciousness, we experience a change in our sense of time:[49]

i. Until we leave our family of origin (at around 18), we are protected by our parents, but we are also constrained by them, never quite believing that we shall escape from our family world. It's like being in a timeless capsule: 'the future is a fantasy space that may possibly not exist'.[50] But we begin to glimpse an endless future, an infinite amount of time ahead of us *provided* we're not suddenly snatched back into the restricted world of our childhood.

ii. Once into our 20s, we're more confident that we have separated from the family, but we haven't yet formed a coherent early-adult life structure.[51]

iii. By the end of our 20s, our sense of time incorporates our adult *past* as well as future; the future is neither infinite nor linear and we must choose between different branches because there isn't time to take them all.

iv. From our mid-30s to mid-40s, there develops a sense of urgency that time is running out. We also have an emotional awareness of our own mortality (see Chapter 6) which, once attained, is never far from consciousness. How time is spent becomes a matter of great importance. We also begin to question whether our 'prize' − freedom from parental restrictions − has been worth it − or even if it exists!

When we replace child with adult consciousness, we replace 'I am theirs' with 'I own myself'; this frees us from the struggle for status, and we are free to acknowledge our mysterious, indelible 'me' as the core of the rest of our life, allowing us to face disappointment, ill-health, and pain with greater strength.

The ages 35–45 have been described as the *midlife passage*, 'the midpoint of life', the 'halfway mark', in which we reexamine our journey up to that point and ask ourselves why we're doing what we're doing and what I really believe in.[52]

> Underneath this vague feeling is the fact, as yet unacknowledged, that there is a down side to life ... and that *I have only so much time before the dark to find my own truth.*[53]

This refers to what has come to be called the 'midlife crisis' (although there's much disagreement as to whether this is a real, distinct, phenomenon). These years have been described as the 'apostrophe in time between the end of growing up and the beginning of growing old ...'.[54]

> The change in time sense forces each of us to a major task of midlife. All our notions of the future need to be rebalanced around the idea of time left to live.[55]

5. *Dream time.* The dream that I describe below seems to capture both the nature of dreams and the nature of time.

> I was sitting at a long table, as in a restaurant, with a number of other people. The only person I actually 'saw' (recognized) was John (someone I've known since childhood, a few years older than myself and a close friend of my older brother, Paul). Not their real names. I had a sense that Paul was also there and that he was one of those, including John, engaged in a conversation, seated away from me on my left-hand side. I felt rather isolated within the group.
>
> Turning to my right, I looked out of a window overlooking the street. A small group of men were gathered around a car and one of them emerged, struggling to keep hold of a rather flimsy, over-filled cardboard box; the box contained John's ashes and as the man tried to keep hold of this precarious box, the ashes began to spill out behind him onto the road.
>
> I remember feeling quite alarmed at what I was witnessing – not because John was in the room and alive and talking – but because I didn't want the man to drop the box or for it to break and empty its contents all over the road.

The dream demonstrates very nicely what Freud called the 'day residues', images from the day's waking/conscious activities which become incorporated into the dream's *manifest content* (what 'happens' in the dream and what we remember about it and report to others).[56] That day, I'd been to the vet to collect our dog's month's supply of food, which was presented to me in a quite unsuitable cardboard box; it was put in my car for me, but I had to bring it into the house when I got home, struggling a little like the man in the dream.

The striking feature of the dream relates to the simultaneity of two events or experiences which, in real life, couldn't possibly have taken place: John's presence in the restaurant and his ashes being carried across the road. In dreams, the usual logic of waking life, including the sequence of events, their duration, their coincidence, and, indeed, their very possibility, is suspended. While we may dismiss dreams as meaningless sleep-related experiences, precisely because of their (apparent) breach of all the rules of normal everyday experience (including the laws of nature), it's this that makes them so fascinating and informative. In dreams, the usual rules and laws don't apply; this reflects their *meaning* (or *latent content*), which is what Freud was mainly interested in. So, in 'dream-time', things can happen together which in 'real life' they couldn't, or the usual sequence of events can follow a different pattern.

While the manifest content requires *description*, the latent content requires *interpretation*; while the former is relatively straightforward (and depends on memory), the latter is much more of a challenge (partly because there's no way of telling if the interpretation is 'right'').

6. *Biological (brain or body) time.* The late biologist John Gibbon described time as the 'primordial context':[57] a fact of life that has been felt by all organisms in every era. In the human body, *biological clocks* keep track of days, months, and years; cellular chronometers (or 'time-pieces') may even determine when we die. As we shall see in Chapter 3, one kind of biological clock in the brain marks much shorter time spans – of seconds to hours. This 'stopwatch' is related to our *experience* of time under different conditions (see Chapter 4).

NOTES

1. William James (1890), p. 225
2. Ibid. (p. 230)
3. Ibid. (p. 231)
4. Ibid. (p. 234)
5. Ibid. (p. 237)
6. Eiser (1994)
7. Fancher & Rutherford (2012), p. 317
8. Pinker (2007), p. 188
9. Rovelli (2018), p.1
10. Callender (2012, p. 15)
11. Ibid. (p. 15)
12. Callender (2012, p. 16)
13. Rochat (2022)
14. Newton (1687); p. 48; emphasis added
15. Ibid. (p. 410; emphasis added)
16. Callender op cit.
17. Rovelli op cit.
18. Ibid. (p. 168)
19. Ibid. (p. 168)
20. Callender op cit.
21. Rovelli op cit. (p. 169)
22. Bergson (1889), p. 104 quoted in Power (2021), p. 107
23. Rochat op cit. (p. 21)
24. Ibid.
25. Ibid.
26. Heidegger (1927/2008)
27. Rochat op cit.
28. Heidegger (1935/1983), p. 90
29. Rovelli op cit. (p. 161)
30. Ibid.
31. Rochat op cit.
32. Ibid. (p. 124; emphasis added)
33. Jones (2019)
34. Pinker op cit. (see Gross, 2023)

35. *Ibid.* (p. 160)

36. Hirschfeld & Gelman (1994)

37. Kant (1781/1998) (A30/B46)

38. Rochat *op cit.* (p. 80)

39. For example, Draaisma (2004); Hammond (2012)

40. For example, Weardon in Fox (2009)

41. For example, Eaglemn in Fox (2009)

42. For example, Wolfradt (2005)

43. Corballis & Suddendorf (2007); Suddendorf & Corballis (2007); Suddendorf et al. (2022)

44. Suddendorf et al., *op cit.*

45. *Psalms* 90 (verse 10)

46. Brown (2007)

47. Dong et al. (2016)

48. See Gross (2020)

49. Gould (1978, 1980)

50. *Ibid.* (1980, p. 35)

51. In the terms used by Levinson et al. (1978) in their *Seasons of a Man's Life*

52. Sheehy (1976)

53. *Ibid.* (p. 350; emphasis in original)

54. *Ibid.* (p. 353)

55. *Ibid.* (p. 353)

56. Freud (1900)

57. As cited in Wright (2006)

2

LANGUAGE AND TIME
MEANING AND METAPHOR

We are so immersed in, and surrounded by, time, that we're often unaware of it. The extent of this immersion is reflected in the number and diversity of English words that refer to time in one way or another. Some examples include:

Before, during, after; when; past; present; future; soon; next; duration, simultaneous

In the days leading up to/following ...

Same time, same place
We're counting down to ...
How long ago did ...?
How recently have ...?
When exactly/approximately did this take place?
If I ever catch you saying that again ...'
I'll love you forever
How much longer must I wait?
How long before you give me your answer?
This feels like history repeating itself

DOI: 10.4324/97810326

Let bigones be bigones
She won't last the night
How long is it likely to last?

With one exception, none of the examples above uses the word 'time'.

Clearly, we keep track of time through the use of 'time-language'; this includes both (1) words that relate to the *cyclical recurrence* of days, months, years, etc. (and see the discussion of *developmental time* in Chapter 1) and (2) those that denote the *linear sequence* of events that make up the flow of life.[1]

Many uses of time-related language take the form of *metaphors*: the *non-literal* use of words. Metaphor is a fundamental mechanism of mind, allowing us to use what we know about the physical and social worlds to help us understand other aspects of our experience; metaphors can help shape our perceptions and actions – often without us being aware of them.[2]

The example of The 'Time is Money' metaphor, which has wide 'currency' (there's another one!) in Western, capitalist countries. This is but one demonstration of how time is conceptualized differently in different cultures (see Chapter 5).[3]

TIME IS MONEY

You're *wasting* my time.
This gadget will *save* you hours.
I don't *have* the time to *give* you.
How do you *spend* your time these days?
That flat tyre *cost* me an hour.
I've *invested* a lot of time in her.
I don't *have enough* time to *spare* for that.
You're *running out* of time.
You need to *budget* your time.
Put *aside* some time for …
Is that *worth your while*?

He's living on *borrowed* time.
Do you *have* much time left?
I *lost* a lot of time when I got sick.
Thank you for your time.
    (Lakoff & Johnson, 1980, pp. 7–8)

Time is a valuable 'commodity' (another one!), a limited 'resource' (and again!) that we use to accomplish our goals. Because of how the concept of 'work' has evolved in modern Western culture – where work is typically associated with the time it takes and where time is precisely measured – we're commonly paid by the hour, week or month. If we break the law, we may repay our debt to society by 'serving time'.[4]

The metaphorical concepts 'Time is money', 'Time is a resource', and 'Time is a valuable commodity' form a *single system* based on *subcategorization relationships*: the first entails the second, and the second entails the third. These practices (being hourly paid in money etc.) are relatively new in the history of human beings and are by no means universal.

They have arisen in modern industrialized societies and structure our basic everyday activities in a very profound way. Corresponding to the fact that we *act* as if time is a valuable *commodity* – a limited resource, even money – we *conceive* of time *that* way ... we understand and experience time as the kind of thing *that* can be spent, wasted, budgeted, invested wisely or poorly, saved, or squandered.[5]

'How do you spend your time?' is usually taken to refer to 'what do we do with our time?' or 'how do you pass your time?'. But each of these questions has quite different connotations: 'What we do with our time' could be understood as 'what activities we engage in' (during a particular time period), while how we pass the time may imply that any activities we engage in aren't important ends in themselves but a means to an end (as in 'killing time' until a certain event takes place)

While 'do with' is much more positive and proactive than 'how we pass', the focus in each case is on the doing or the passing, 'how we spend time' focuses much more on time as a commodity (see above). When we talk about spending money, we're describing an *exchange* of money for any number of goods, services, or activities (be it clothes, smartphones, repairs to the washing machine, concert tickets, etc.). In the case of spending time, a comparable kind of exchange is taking place: here, money is replaced by time which is then used *as* if it were money. Time is a finite resource (as is money), which we exchange for ('spend') on one or more of these same goods, services, or activities.

This analysis suggests that not only is time money, but also money is time: they're interchangeable in that while both are finite – and highly valued – resources, their value isn't an inherent feature (they're not precious *in and of themselves*); rather, it lies in what they enable us to do or have in exchange.

TALKING ABOUT TIME, SPACE, AND CAUSALITY

As we noted in Chapter 1, 'time' can be defined – and measured – in several different ways (some more 'objective' than others). One relates to the *sequence of events*: our perception of the world involves certain things occurring *before* or *after* others, as when thunder usually precedes lightning (and both precede the rain), and divorce only occurs following marriage. While the former is a natural phenomenon, the latter is, of course, socio-cultural; also, the intervals of time *between* the events and their respective *duration* are significantly different. While it's relatively easy to infer that the thunder and lightning in some way *cause* the rain to occur (the former two *precede* the latter), it doesn't make a lot of sense to claim that marriage *causes* divorce. Invariably, rain does follow thunder and lightning, but not every marriage ends in divorce.

So, the *order* in which things occur sometimes tells us about what things cause certain other things (effects). When someone hits your patella (knee-cap) in just the right place, the knee-jerk reflex is produced (your knee shoots, uncontrollably, into the air); together with the brevity of the events, we can quite easily infer that the former causes the latter. Striking the patella is a *necessary and sufficient condition* (cause) of the knee-jerk reflex (effect): it won't occur without someone striking your patella, but, if they do, the reflex is certain to occur. However, marriage is only a *necessary condition* of divorce: you must first be married, but there's no guarantee that divorce will occur.

What we can conclude from this discussion is that time-related words, such as 'before', 'after', 'follow', 'precede', and 'simultaneous', tell us how different events occur *in relation to each other*; rather than perceiving and understanding the world in terms of a series of discrete, unrelated events or experiences, we try to explain one thing in terms of another (such as cause – and – effect). Implicitly, we take events to be related in particular ways: the past can influence the future but not vice-versa (but can the future affect the present?), and events that last a very short time – or which occurred a considerable time ago - are unlikely to trigger those that unfold over substantial periods of time – or which are relatively recent.

As we noted in Chapter 1, time as defined in Einstein's relativity theories couldn't be much more different from our everyday experience of time. However, one aspect of Einstein's theory does have a counterpart in the psychology of time (at least as expressed in language), namely, the *deep equivalence of time with space*.[6]

We routinely use space to represent time in calendars, hour-glasses, and other time-keeping devices. The cognitive similarity also shows up in everyday metaphors where spatial terms are 'borrowed' to refer to time. A number of examples of *conceptual metaphors* have been identified (see the 'Time is Money' example above).[7]

- *Time orientation*: an observer in the 'present' has the past behind and the future in front, as in 'That's all behind us'; 'We're looking ahead'; 'She has a great future in front of her'.

- Metaphorical motion can be added in one of two ways: (1) time is a parade that sweeps past a stationary observer (moving time); e.g. 'The time will come when …'; The time for action has arrived'; 'The deadline is approaching'; 'The summer is flying by'. (2) the landscape of time is stationary and the observer proceeds through it (moving observer); e.g. 'There's trouble down the road'; 'We're coming up to Christmas'; 'She left at nine o'clock'; 'We passed the deadline'; 'We're halfway through the semester'.

These two metaphors are incompatible (despite both using space for time); this explains why statements like 'Let's move the meeting ahead a week' are ambiguous: it can mean (a) 'make it earlier' (as in (1)) or (b) 'make it later' (as in (2)). 'Wednesday's meeting has been moved forward two days' can mean that it has been switched to Monday, because if one invokes the time-as-procession metaphor, 'forward' is aligned with the march of time toward oneself – an event that has been moved forward in the procession of days is now closer to us. Or, it could mean that it's been switched to Friday: if one invokes the time-as-landscape metaphor, 'forward' is aligned with one's own marching through time – we have to walk further, past more days, to get to an event that has been moved to a forward position.[8]

People can be 'tilted' (another one) towards one or other interpretation if they have recently read a sentence that is compatible with only one of the metaphors, such as 'We passed the deadline two days ago' (which creates a bias towards the 'Friday' interpretation) or 'The deadline passed two days ago' (which creates a Monday bias).[9]

Taking this logic a step further, it has been shown that an actual experience of motion – not just words using a motion metaphor – can tip people's interpretations of the ambiguous 'forward' one way or another. If asked to imagine pushing an office chair, this creates a bias towards the 'Friday' interpretation (it coincides with their own march through the metaphorical landscape) or pulling the chair towards them with a string creates a 'Monday' bias, where it coincides with time's advance towards them.[10]

Although the use of space to represent time appears to be universal, how time is aligned with a dimension of space can vary. In English alone, (1) and (2) coexist with time as a pursuer ('Old age overtook him') and with time rotated to the vertical ('Traditions were handed down to them from their ancestors').[11] Two striking examples of the space-for-time metaphor are: (a) In Chinese, vertical metaphors for time are even more common: earlier events are 'up' and later events 'down'; (b) In Aymara (spoken in the Andes), the time-orientation metaphor is turned 180 degrees: the future is said to be 'behind' one and the past 'in front'.[12] (See Chapter 5 for a discussion of other cultural differences.)

Language is saturated with implicit metaphors, such as *events are objects* and *time is space*; indeed, metaphor is so commonplace in language that it's difficult to find expressions for abstract ideas that *aren't* metaphorical.[13] However, even a metaphor as common as *time is space* doesn't depend on the concept of time 'actually camping out in the neural real estate used by the concept of space'[14] (a phrase itself full of colourful metaphors). Some brain-damaged patients can lose their ability to understand prepositions for space, such as 'She's at the corner' and 'She ran through the forest', while retaining their ability to understand the same prepositions for time, as in 'She arrived at 1.30' and 'She worked through the evening'. Other patients showed the *opposite* pattern. This suggests that different brain circuits are responsible for understanding space and for understanding time.[15]

In addition to metaphor, and in an even deeper way, time can be related to space (and substance) through the *semantics of tense and verbs*.

1.   We're familiar with tense (and is captured in the arrow of time image, with the past preceding the present and the present

preceding the future): tense depicts the 'location' of an event or state (e.g. 'She loved you'; 'She loves you'; 'She will love you'). 'The best way to understand the language of time is to depict it, naturally enough, in space ...'[16]

2. 'Aspect' (a general realm of meaning which depicts how events and states are distributed in time, how they unfold over time, their 'shape'). E.g. while 'Swat a fly' is conceptualized as instantaneous (within the 'specious present'[17]: see Chapter 3), 'run around' is open-ended, and 'draw a circle' culminates in an event that marks the act's completion. 'Aspect' can also express the viewpoint on an event: 'She was climbing the tree' suggests being there when this happened (viewed from the' inside'), while 'She climbed the tree' suggests viewing from the 'outside'.[18] (This might represent a stylistic difference – and not necessarily a difference of aspect (or both). 'She was climbing the tree ...' creates a more dramatic effect, setting up an expectation that something else then took place (captured in the use of 'when' which almost invariably will follow 'tree'; by contrast, 'She climbed the tree' is more mundane, doesn't necessarily create any expectations, and uses the straightforward past tense of the verb to climb. 'Climbing' is a gerund (made from a verb and used as a noun) neither a simple past tense, nor a straightforward present tense; it's somewhere in-between the past and the present.)

DIFFERENCES BETWEEN TIME AND SPACE

Another way in which time and space words are related is where time is substituted for distance: if someone asks you how far you live from the railway station, you may reply by saying "just a five-minute walk". However, if you were asked how long it takes to get to the station from your house, you're unlikely to say "About half a mile", suggesting that time is a more pervasive form of human thought (or intuitive category) – at least among English speakers – than space/distance.

While the past is frozen and cannot be changed (except in science fiction like Back to the Future), the future is a mere potentiality and can be altered by the choices we make in the present.[19] (However, not everyone would agree: 'history' is often being 're-written' in the sense that new evidence regarding past events may suggest new/modified interpretations. Also, as in George Orwell's (1949) famous dystopian novel, Nineteen Eighty Four, the past is literally 'spliced' as in editing a movie in order to make it consistent with the Party's latest version of history. The protagonist, Winston Smith, works for the Ministry of Truth and his job is to edit the past.)

The view of the past as fixed, etc. is reflected in how many languages make only a two-way distinction between past and non-past, the latter embracing both present and future. Many languages don't denote the future in the tense system at all; instead, they distinguish between events that have actually taken place or are now taking place (realis), and those that are hypothetical, generic, or in the future (irrealis).[20] This distinction underlies the Aymara metaphor in which the past and future are reversed compared with what English tells us: the past has already taken place and is knowable – it can be seen before our eyes – while the future is 'up for grabs and is inscrutable, as if it were out of view'.[21]

Kant, time, and language

While most of us – including psychologists, other scientists, philosophers, etc. – implicitly believe in an external world that exists independently of us, known to us through our sense organs, we can only grasp the world through the structures of our minds; this means, according to Kant, that we cannot truly know the world in itself (see Chapter 1). However, while we cannot directly know the world but only indirectly through some kind of mind, at least the human mind allows us to understand the world well enough for science and technological applications of that scientific knowledge to proceed.

As we noted in Chapter 1, Newton believed that 'absolute, true and mathematical time, of itself, and from its own nature flows equally without relation to anything'.[22] But for Kant (1781/1998; 1783/1950), the concept of time – and space – are the mind's supports for negotiating reality.

> Languages appear to be organized by Kantian abstract categories. We see them in the basic parts of speech: substance in nouns, space in prepositions, causality in verbs, time in verbs and in markers for tense ...[23]

However, as we noted in Chapter 1, many physicists today argue that space and time – in the sense of empty 'media' into which objects are slotted – don't exist. The 'reality' of time is perhaps easier to grasp in a *biological* context (particularly, in relation to the brain: see Chapter 3.)

NOTES

1. Pinker (2007)
2. Lakoff & Johnson (1980)
3. Ibid.
4. Ibid.
5. Ibid. (p. 8)
6. Pinker op cit.
7. Lakoff & Johnson op cit.
8. Ibid.
9. Boroditsky (2000); Boroditsky & Ramscar (2002)
10. Ibid.
11. Pinker op cit.
12. Ibid.
13. Ibid.
14. Ibid. (p. 250)
15. Kemmerer (2005)
16. Pinker op cit. (p. 193)

17. James (1890)
18. Pinker *op cit*.
19. *Ibid*.
20. *Ibid*.
21. *Ibid*. (p. 196)
22. Kant (1687), cited in Korner (1955)
23. Pinker *op cit*. (p. 159)

3

BIOLOGICAL TIME
INTERNAL TICKING CLOCKS

The late biologist, John Gibbon, described time as the'primordial context':[1] a fact of life that has been felt by all organisms in every era. In the human body, *biological clocks* keep track of days, months and years; *cellular chronometers* (or 'time-pieces') may even determine when we die. As we shall see below, there's one kind of biological clock in the brain that marks much shorter time intervals of seconds to hours. Because this so-called 'stopwatch' is related to our *experience* of time under different conditions, we'll discuss it in Chapter 4 in relation to 'mind time'.

> For all the advances of modern society, we cannot afford to ignore the rhythms of the animal brain within us, any more than we can neglect our need to breathe or eat. Without the biological clocks in our brains, our lives would be chaotic, our actions disorganized. The brain has internalized the rhythms of Nature, but can tick on for months without sight of the sun.[2]

Box 3.1 describes some important bodily rhythms.

DOI: 10.4324/9781032696218-3

Box 3.1 Some major bodily rhythms

- A bodily rhythm is a cyclical variation over some period of time in physiological and psychological processes.
- Many human activities take place within a cycle of about 24 hours (circadian rhythms: 'circa' = 'about'; 'diem' = 'day').
- Rhythms that have a cycle longer than 24 hours are called infradian rhythms (such as the human menstrual cycle).
- Circannual rhythms are yearly rhythms and are a subset of infradian rhythms. Examples include changes in the seasons as these relate to where the sun sits in the sky (low in winter, high in summer, etc.). Early humans, by recognizing that the sun follows an annual cycle of rising and setting in the same places each year, could accurately anticipate upcoming seasonal changes and coordinate their affairs accordingly.[3] Circannual rhythms regulate behaviours such as bird migration and hibernation of a range of mammals; some non-human animals are so attuned to the sun that they completely lose their bearings in the rare event of a solar eclipse.
- Ultradian rhythms last less than 24 hours, a major example being the 90–120 minute cycle of human sleep stages.[4]
- Environmental factors such as light-dark cycles, noise, and clocks that provide clues to these internal rhythms are called exogenous (i.e. external) zeitgebers (German for 'time-givers'). In the absence of any zeitgebers, behaviours that show rhythmical alternation/periodicity are controlled by internal timing devices – internal biological clocks (or endogenous pacemakers).

CIRCADIAN RHYTHMS

Most animals display a circadian rhythm, which tunes our bodies to the cycles of sunlight and darkness caused by the earth's rotation; it helps to program the daily habit of sleeping at night and waking in the morning. During a 24-hour period, there's a cycle of several physiological functions (heart rate, breathing rate, body temperature, hormonal secretion, urine excretion, immune function, alertness, etc.); these tend to reach maximum values during the late afternoon/early evening and minimum values in the early hours of the morning.

This internal clock is as reliable as most manufactured ones: the rhythm deviates by no more than a few minutes over several months. It runs without the need for a stimulus from the external environment (zeitgebers), as dramatically demonstrated by pioneering studies of the internal clock. (See Box 3.2.)

Box 3.2   The internal clock ticks underground

- In 1938, two American researchers spent 32 days and nights in Mammoth Cave, Kentucky, one of the deepest, darkest caverns on earth.[5] Two ground-breaking findings were that (i) humans generate their own *endogenous* circadian rhythm in the absence of sunlight; and (ii) their reliably-repeating wake/sleep cycles were consistently *longer* than 24 hours.[6]

- It's now widely agreed that the average duration of the human endogenous circadian clock is 24 hours and 15 minutes.[7]

- In the 1960s, Aschoff (the founder of *chronobiology*, the scientific study of humans' internal clocks) conducted experiments in a disused bunker. For several weeks, his participants lived in isolation, collecting their own urine and monitoring their body temperatures; no time clues or zeitgebers were allowed.

- While participants still tended to sleep for eight hours, their awake time stretched slightly beyond 16 hours; this revealed an internal clock that ran 20 minutes *slower* than the 24-hour day. Each day they went to sleep later and later until they were entirely out of synch with the rhythms of normal life.[8]

- In 1962, Michel Siffre, then a young French cave explorer (and now a chronobiologist) spent 63 days, 130 metres underground in the French Alps. He was deprived of all indicators of time; his only connection to the outside world was a phone line to a camp above ground that he called on waking and prior to going to sleep, providing details of pulse rate, body temperature, and other physiological measures.

- His sleep-wake cycle increased to 24 hours and 30 minutes, falling asleep and waking a little later each day until he had become nocturnal.

- In 1972, Siffre spent six months underground in Midnight Cave, Texas – the longest period of timelessness attempted up to that point. He wore electrodes on his scalp and body to monitor his physiological activity and performed daily cognitive tasks. He achieved a 48-hour cycle twice.

- Finally, in 2000, now aged 60, Siffre decided to explore the effects of ageing on the body clock. After two months in a French cave, his cycle had evolved as it had in 1962 – when he was 23.

- Siffre's efforts inspired a line of research, culminating in a 2017 Nobel Prize for the three researchers who identified the genes governing our multiple body clocks. They also contributed to the invention of light therapy for mood disorders and drugs to treat jet lag.[9]

Circadian patterns are expressed in every cell of the body: confined to a petri dish under constant lighting, human cells still follow a 24-hour cycle of *gene* activity, hormone secretion, and energy production. The cycles are hardwired, varying by as little as one per cent – just minutes per day.[10]

While light isn't required to establish a circadian cycle, it is needed to *synchronize* the phase of the hardwired clock with natural day and night cycles. Like an ordinary clock that runs a few minutes fast or slow each day, the circadian clock needs to be continually reset to stay accurate.[11] So, how is the internal (biological) clock reset each day to the cycle of the real (external) world, and where can the clock be found?

The clock is believed to be a tiny cluster of about 3,000 neurons, the *suprachiasmatic nucleus* (SCN), located in the medial hypothalamus. Damage to the SCN in rats causes their circadian rhythm to completely disappear: the sleep-wake cycle, eating and drinking, hormone secretion, etc. become totally random within a 24-hour period.

Most of what's known about the SCN is based on experiments using *ablation* with non-human animals: parts of the brain are surgically removed. Anatomical studies involving humans have shown that we too have an SCN;[12] its function is to synchronize all the bodily functions governed by the circadian rhythm.

The SCN is situated directly above the optic chiasma (the junction of the two optic nerves en route to the brain). A tuft of thin nerve fibres branches off from the main nerve and penetrates the hypothalamus above, forming synaptic connections with cells in the SCN. This anatomically insignificant pathway is the link between the outside world and the brain's own clock.[13] So, the retina (at the back of the eye) projects directly onto the SCN; this ensures that the sleep-wake cycle is tuned to the rhythm of night and day; if this connection with the retina is cut, the cycle goes 'haywire'.

The SCN also tells the brain's *pineal gland*, situated near the corpus callosum (which links the two cerebral hemispheres), to release *melatonin* (the 'sleep hormone' or 'draught'). Melatonin promotes sleep in humans and is secreted only at night. In response to daylight, the SCN emits signals that stop the *paraventricular nucleus* from producing a message that would ultimately result in the release of melatonin.

CONSCIOUSNESS AND TIME PERCEPTION

> The idea of our body – and the related concept of space – might seem to be the most deeply 'plumbed-in' concept we have. But in fact there is another concept that is even more taken for granted by humans: that of time. Like space, it seems absurd to think of time as an idea. It seems just to be. But if that were the case – if time proceeded at its stately pace without any conceptual input – it would pass at the same pace for each of us, whatever our circumstances and whatever the conditions of our brains. And that is not the case …[14]

Carter is describing mind time. As we have noted in Chapter 1, our experience of time depends on a number of factors, including age (see Chapter 6), the nature of the situation (see Chapter 4), and the state of our brains (see below); the latter can denote both abnormalities (caused by disease or accident: see Chapter 4) and the way that the normal, intact, brain functions. Similarly:

> 'Mind time' has to do with how we experience the passage of time and how we organize chronology. Despite the steady beat of the clock, duration can seem fast or slow, short or long. And this variability can happen on different scales, from decades, seasons, weeks and hours, down to the tiniest intervals of music – the span of a note or the moment of silence between two notes. We also place events in time, deciding when they occurred, in which order, and on what scale, whether that of a lifetime or of a few seconds.[15]

Complementing these different examples is the distinction between (a) perception of time: the experience of brief intervals of time, grasped as a single unit – and relatively unaffected by memory;

and (b) *retention of time*: the *retrospective* experience of longer time intervals – and assumed to be affected by memory.[16]

DISCRETE VISUAL FRAMES

Perhaps the most fundamental question being investigated by neuroscientists is whether our perception of the world is continuous or a series of discrete snapshots, like frames on a film strip. If we understood this, then perhaps we would be able to explain how the healthy brain works out the chronological order of the mass events that bombard our senses.[17]

Some of the first hints that we may perceive the world through discrete 'frames' arrived with studies of the well-known 'wagon-wheel illusion': the wheels of a forward-moving vehicle appear to slow down or even roll backwards. The illusion was first noted during the playback of old Westerns and is produced by the fact that the camera takes a sequence of snapshots of the wheel as it rotates: if the speed of rotation is right, it can look as if each spoke has rotated a small distance *backwards* with each frame, when in actual fact they have moved *forwards*. Typically, each frame captured by the camera shows the wheel after just under a quarter of a revolution.

This effect isn't confined to the movies: people also report experiencing it in real life. If these observations could be reproduced in the laboratory, it would suggest that the brain naturally slices our visual perception into a succession of snapshots.[18]

The illusion was experimentally recreated: when the wheel was spun at particular speeds, all the participants reported seeing it turn the 'wrong' way.[19] This suggests that the continuity of our perceptual experience *is itself an illusion*. The researchers proposed a visual frame rate of 13 frames per second. What in the brain determines this rate? (see Box 3.3).

However, the case for discrete perception is far from 'proven'.[21] Participants were shown a pair of overlapping patterns, both moving at the same rate. They often reported seeing one pattern

Box 3.3 Discrete visual frames and the right inferior parietal lobe

- Participants' brain waves were measured using an *electro-encephalogram* (EEG) and found a specific rhythm (a 13-hertz wave) in the right inferior parietal lobe (RIPL). This is normally associated with perception of visual location.[20]

- It seemed plausible that as this wave oscillates (moves up and down), the RIPL's receptivity to new visual information also oscillates, leading to something comparable to discrete visual frames.

- To test this hypothesis, the researchers used transcranial magnetic stimulation, a non-invasive technique that can interfere with – and block – activity in specific brain areas; this is aimed at disrupting the regular brain wave in the RIPL.

- The effect of this disruption was to inhibit the periodic sampling of visual frames that's crucial for seeing the wagon wheel illusion: the probability of seeing it was reduced by 30 per cent.

- However, participants could still see the regular motion of the wheels, probably because other brain regions, which don't operate at the necessary 13 hertz, took over some of the motion perception.

- Van Rullen et al. call the RIPL the 'when' pathway: it plays a critical role in timing perceptual events relative to one another.

reversing independently of the other, suggesting that they *weren't* taking frames of the world (otherwise, *everything* would have to reverse together, at the same time).[22]

However, could it be that the brain processes different objects within the visual field *independently* of each other, even if they overlap in space?[23] The RPIL may well be taking the 'snapshots' of the two moving patterns at *separate* moments – and possibly at slightly different rates – making it plausible that the illusions could happen independently for each object. This implies that, rather than a single 'roll of film', the brain processes *several* separate streams, each recording a separate piece of information.

This way of dealing with incoming information may also apply to other forms of perception, such as object or sound recognition. This possibility was investigated in a study of *near-threshold luminance detection*. Participants were exposed to flashes of light barely bright enough to consciously perceive: the likelihood of them consciously noticing the flash depended on the phase of *another* wave in the front of the brain, which rises and falls about seven times per second. When this second wave was near its trough (or fall), participants were more likely to see the flash; when it was close to its peak, they were more likely to miss it. These findings suggest that there's a succession of 'on' and 'off' periods of perception: attention involves collecting information through snapshots.[24]

If, as it appears, each separate neural process that governs our perception is recorded in its own stream of discrete frames, we need to ask how all these streams might combine to give us a consistent, coherent picture of the world? After all, we don't perceive a series of unrelated, fragmented snapshots: we perceive complete, discrete *objects* and *people* and *events*. Try to imagine what it would be like if we were unable to piece together a chronological sequence of sensory events?

Since light travels faster than sound, there's actually a minuscule gap (in the brain) between the visual stimulus of, say, a cup hitting the floor and breaking and hearing the sound of it breaking;[25] without some sort of *grouping system* we might see the cup smashing *before* we hear it happen.[26] But, usually, we experience these as happening simultaneously.

Again, consider what experience would be like if different moments of consciousness were discrete, such that what we experienced at each moment wasn't *temporally connected* (connected in time) to what we'd experienced just before.[27] In other words, what if different moments were *discontinuous*, separated in time from each other?

THE BUILDING BLOCKS OF CONSCIOUSNESS

According to the *building blocks of consciousness hypothesis* (BBCH), all the separate snapshots from the senses may feed into blocks of information (the 'building blocks of consciousness') within a higher processing stream; these building blocks underlie our perception of time. If two events fall into the same building block, they're perceived *simultaneously* (different aspects of the *same* events, such as the smashing cup); but if they fall into separate, consecutive blocks, they're perceived as *successive* (two *distinct* events).[28]

An interval of 30–50 milliseconds (m/sec: thousandth of a second) is necessary to bring together the distributed activity within the neural system into a single time window. In one experiment, participants' reaction times (RTs) were analysed by measuring how quickly their eyes moved to follow a dot jumping across a computer screen; their RTs seemed to follow a 30-m/sec cycle. If the dot moved at any point within this cycle, it took until the end of the interval before any response occurred.[29] A similar cycle has been observed when participants are asked to judge whether an auditory and a visual stimulus are simultaneous or consecutive.[30]

Complementing this 30-m/sec cycle is a *dopamine loop*. The notion of flowing time is encoded in a neural circuit fuelled by the neurotransmitter dopamine: each 'loop' of activity takes, on average, 1/10th of a second to complete (i.e. 100 m/secs.) and events registered by the brain within a single loop are experienced as a *single occurrence*.[31]

WHAT/WHEN IS 'NOW'?

The brain's registration of events within a single loop as a single occurrence is, in turn, related to our sense of 'the present'/'now' (what William James (1890) called the 'saddle-back' of duration or the 'specious present').

The term 'the remembered present' is meant to highlight how consciousness arises from the dynamic, ongoing interaction between the brain and the environment; this, in turn, is based on the *recategorization* of present and past experience.[32] While our subjective sense of the passing moment is unified, the neural mechanisms responsible are extremely diverse, complex, massively parallel (involving several different neural operations simultaneously), and involve many interacting brain loci (especially the thalamus and cortex). The dopamine loop is part of the concept of an *interval timer* (IT) (see below).

Our normal idea of the present moment corresponds to one of the 'temporal packets' or 'ticks' of the internal clock: about 1/10th–1/5th of a second. Each tick is the time it takes for the electrical nerve impulse to travel around a loop of dopamine-producing neurons. All the information we process during that time window is experienced as happening *simultaneously*; this allows us to perceive the smashing cup (see above) as a single incident. This has been called a 'smearing' of time, fleshing out the subjective moment by squashing into it all the events that fall into a particular time packet.[33]

However, the downside of this 'smearing'/'squashing' is that each of our moments is slightly blurred – sometimes literally:

> When we watch the beating of a fly's wings, we cannot see each individual flap because several of them happen in each of our time windows. The result is that we see a fuzzy haze rather than a clear outline of a moving wing. If our subjective concept of time was more fine-grained, allowing us to split each moment into many more parts, we would see things more clearly ...[34]

We probably didn't evolve a more fine-grained sense of time because this would have produced information overload; after all, what advantage is there to seeing the individual beats of a fly's wing?

> The things we need to discriminate most clearly are those that happen in seconds (animals moving or, today, cars bearing down on us) ... not milliseconds ... Only when we are faced with a life-threatening situation, or one which is wildly exciting, can we afford to ignore everything in the past and future and concentrate on the present moment. And when that happens, our brains oblige by breaking the moment into more parts so each one can be separately scrutinized and dealt with.[35]

As conveyed by the concept of the *stream of consciousness*,[36] consciousness has a changing yet continuous character: if different moments were separate and unconnected, although we may still perceive a world of stable objects, there'd be no coherence to our experience (see above):

> We would experience a flash of existence at a time, and this flash would not be integrated with the previous moment or the next one. One might think that this discontinuous strobe-like existence would require that we remember from one moment to the next what we have experienced and make judgements that would somehow summarise or collate the succession of moments into a coherent object. But if consciousness were genuinely discontinuous, so would be our memory and our judgement ...[37]

Such experience has been likened to James's 'blooming, buzzing confusion'[38] (which was actually meant to describe a newborn baby's perceptual experience); for example, we'd be unable to experience a movement or a melody as it develops.[39]

The Austro-German philosopher Edmund Husserl worked out a description of how it's possible to actually hear a melody, see a movement, or perceive identity over time. One moment of consciousness isn't disconnected from the previous one or the next. If things appear in a continuous or continually developing way – which they do in normal waking consciousness – then previous phases of experience must in some way be tied together with subsequent ones. Of course, some of the things we experience may themselves be disjointed events, but we still experience an integrated successive flow, rather than a disjointed, stop-and-start progression. If experience weren't like this, then all events would seem disjointed.[40]

But how exactly is one moment of consciousness interconnected with earlier and later ones? Husserl's answer is a detailed account of the structure of internal time-consciousness (see Box 3.4).

Box 3.4   Husserl's account of internal time-consciousness

- As one moment of consciousness fades into the past, we don't call upon memory as a new cognitive act in order to somehow capture that moment. Indeed, even in remembering something our experience is structured as a connected streaming process.
- If we claimed that memory is responsible for retaining the past phases of memory, we'd get stuck in an infinite regress: for every act of remembering, there'd have to be another that allows us to remember the previous one – and so on ad infinitum.
- Rather, implicit in the very nature of consciousness (whether this involves perception, memory, imagination, a train of conceptual thought, etc.) is a binding of one moment to the next (what Husserl calls retention in relation to past moments and protention in relation to the future).
- When saying the word 'on', I also have an anticipatory sense (protention) of where the sentence is going – or, at least, that the sentence is heading towards some kind of

ending. Some form of anticipation seems essential to my experience of speaking in a meaningful way – and is a feature of all normal experience.[41]

- Husserl's model explains not only how the perception of a *temporal object*, such as a melody, is possible (what he calls a *primal impression*), given a changing stream of consciousness, but also how consciousness *unifies itself* across time.[42]

- Since retention retains the entire *just-past* phase – which also includes retention of the *previous* phase – there's a *retentional continuum* that stretches back over prior experience; this maintains the sense of the past moments *in the present*.

Take the example of speaking the sentence 'The cat is on the mat' to illustrate Husserl's account. When I reach the word 'on', I'm no longer saying the previous words, but I – and anyone who's listening to me – still retain a sense of the beginning of the sentence – otherwise, the sentence would make no sense. Retention keeps the intentional sense of the words available even after the words are no longer being spoken. As I'm uttering the sentence, not only do I have a sense of the sentence as it unfolds, but I also have a sense that I am the one who's just spoken the words; this sense of *self* is built into my experience at the very basic level of the *retentional function*: it's the retentional structure of consciousness that makes it possible.[43]

Another way of capturing the nature of 'now is the concept of the *subjective present*[44] and the related *three-second window* (see Box 3.5).

Box 3.5   The subjective present and the three-second window

- As we've seen, Psychologists have been interested in 'the present' as a basic temporal phenomenon since James (1890). According to Pöppel, we're now in a position to assess how long such a subjective present actually lasts: several different experiments converge on the value of 2–3 seconds.

• What's called the three-second window was first described by various researchers in the mid-1800s. For example, this time interval was dubbed the 'point of indifference': participants estimated that tones that were actually *shorter* than three seconds lasted *longer*, while those that were actually *longer* than three seconds were reported as being *shorter*.[45]

• Despite technological and social revolutions, and 'cultural speed-up', this three-second point of indifference has been identified in several different research areas (including time perception proper, speech, movement control, vision, audition, and memory). These findings suggest that the three-second window is hardwired into the brain.[46]

Various species of higher mammals tend to segment their motor behaviour in the same temporal range as humans (2–3 seconds);[49] this suggests that we're dealing with a universal principle of temporal integration that transcends human cognitive and behavioural control.[50] Pöppel also claims that it's impossible to perform two or three different tasks simultaneously with the same degree of concentration. Apparently, simultaneous awareness and processing of information actually occurs within three-second windows, during each of which the brain takes in all the data about the environment as a *block*; subsequent events are then processed in the next window.

This implies that 'multitasking' is more apparent than real. Multitasking is more like surfing between different TV channels: what's really going on is a three-second switch between different tasks, which is quick enough to create the *impression* of simultaneity.[51] During any three-second window, we can only concentrate

Box 3.6   Testing the three-second window for yourself

Figure 3.1 Rubin's vase.

- What do you see in Figure 3.1?
- If you've seen this before, you'll know that there are two different ways of interpreting the image: if you stare at it long enough, it will automatically switch to the alternative (and back again) – but this will usually take just three seconds.
- Try repeating out loud, as fast as you can, the following (meaningless) syllables: 'ku-ba-ku'.
- What happens?
- Usually, eventually, you'll be saying 'kuba' or 'baku'; these will start alternating every three seconds (beyond your control). One or other will 'take possession of conscious content'.[47]
- ('Kuba' is likely to become 'Cuba'; 'Baku' is, in fact, the capital of Azerbaijan).[48]

on or hold one task in the foreground of consciousness. This corresponds to the singular 'state of being conscious' (STOBCON): this describes a universal, omnipresent integrative process that is automatic and pre-semantic (it's not determined by what's processed but defines a temporal window within which conscious activities can take place. It represents a pragmatic definition of the subjective present (see above).[52]

The interval timer

The so-called interval timer (IT) (or 'stopwatch' in the brain) marks time spans of seconds to hours; it helps us work out how fast we need to run to catch a ball, when to applaud our favourite song, and to sense how long we can stay in bed after the alarm has gone off.[53] The IT enlists the higher cognitive power of the cerebral cortex, which controls perception, memory, and conscious thought. (Memory and time is discussed in Chapter 4.)

NOTES

1. Wright (2006)
2. Blakemore (1988), p. 67
3. Suddendorf et al. (2022)
4. See Gross (2020)
5. Kleitman (1939)
6. Ibid.
7. Walker (2017)
8. Gamble (2013)
9. Spinney (2018)
10. Wright op cit.
11. Ibid.
12. Empson (1993)
13. Blakemore op cit.
14. Carter (2006), p. 134; emphasis added)
15. Damasio (2012)
16. Frankenheuser (1959)
17. Fox (2009)
18. Ibid.
19. Van Rullen et al. (2008)
20. Ibid.
21. Fox op cit.
22. Eagleman cited in Fox op cit.
23. Van Rullen (e.g. Busch et al., 2009)
24. Busch et al. (2009)
25. Carter op cit.
26. Fox op cit.
27. Gallagher (2007)
28. Pöppel (2009)
29. Pöppel & Logothetis (1986)
30. Fox op cit.
31. Carter op cit.
32. Edelman (1989)
33. Carter op cit.
34. Ibid. (p. 136)

35. Ibid. (p. 136)
36. James (1890)
37. Gallagher op cit. (p. 690)
38. James op cit.
39. Gallagher op cit.
40. Husserl (1928/1991)
41. Gallagher op cit.
42. Ibid.
43. Ibid.
44. Pöppel (2004)
45. Karl von Vireordt (1868), cited in Colman (2008)
46. Wallisch (2008)
47. Pöppel (2004)
48. Wallisch op cit.
49. Gerstner & Fazio (1995)
50. Pöppel op cit.
51. Manhart (2004)
52. Pöppel (1997)
53. Wright op cit.

4

MIND TIME

SPEEDING UP, SLOWING DOWN, STANDING STILL

It's quite common to hear people express surprise to learn that particular events happened as long ago – or as recently – as they did. There are also well-worn sayings and observations, in English at least, that refer to the relative speed with which time 'travels' ('Time flies when you're having fun'; 'The lecture was so boring it seemed to go on for hours!'; 'I knew I was going to hit the other car and everything seemed to happen in slow motion').

Clearly, in these examples, it's not the events themselves that have speeded up or slowed down in any objective way; rather, it's our *perception* of how long they lasted, or our *judgement* regarding the amount of (real) time that has elapsed since they took place, that we're alluding to.

If these perceptions and judgements were in tune with the actual duration of the events, we wouldn't need to express surprise or make observations about the relative speed of (experienced) time under different conditions. But clearly, these are not always in tune and what this chapter aims to do is to identify some of the major influencing factors on this mis-match, including brain damage, fear, mental disorder, and age; in turn, these can affect both *memory* and our *ability to estimate* (real) *time*.

DOI: 10.4324/9781032696218-4

THE ELASTICITY OF TIME

Despite our minds creating for us an experience of time which both feels mainly smooth and which we can share with others (allowing us to coordinate our activities)

> ... time never stops surprising us. The reason time is so fascinating is that we never appear to become accustomed to the way it seems to play tricks on us. Throughout life, we find it warps ...[1]

TIME ESTIMATION IN THE LABORATORY

An early study was conducted by a husband-and-wife Psychology team, in which they woke sleeping participants and asked them to estimate the time; they were mostly accurate within 15 minutes either way (under or overestimated).

In another early study, participants (undergraduate students) were given a routine task, interrupted at intervals, and then asked to estimate how long had elapsed since the task had begun. For a total clock time of 260 seconds, the average estimate was 398 seconds: the group as a whole produced an average positive error (overestimate) of 138 seconds in their verbal estimations. There were quite dramatic individual differences, ranging from 98–720 seconds.[2]

This 'method of verbal estimation' is one of the standard techniques for laboratory investigation of time. Another is the 'method of production', in which the experimenter decides on a time interval (say, a minute), asks participants to start estimating, and then to stop when they think a minute has elapsed. Unlike verbal estimation, this essentially assesses participants' concept of the specified time interval. Like verbal estimation, the production method produces huge individual differences; when a minute is the chosen interval, individuals differ between 15 and 90 seconds.[3,4]

Four factors have been found to underly the verbal estimation of time:

1. *Interest versus boredom*: the greater the boredom, the longer the estimates.
2. *Filled-time versus empty-time*: longer estimates tended to occur with filled than with empty time.
3. *Repetition*: estimates of the second of two periods of a repeated activity tended to be shorter.
4. *Activity versus passivity*: periods of passivity are estimated as longer than periods of activity.[5]

The elasticity of time is perhaps best appreciated when we are the spectators of a performance (such as a film, play, concert, or lecture). The actual duration of the performance and its subjective duration are different things.[6]

Alfred Hitchcock's 1948 film *Rope*, has been described as a 'technically remarkable work' (p. 46);[7] it was shot in continuous, unedited ten-minute takes. While others have used this method (such as Orson Wells in *Touch of Evil*, Robert Altman in *The Player*, and Martin Scorsese in *GoodFellas*), no other film has used it so consistently as Hitchcock in *Rope*.

Hitchcock was attempting to depict a story that had been told in a play occurring in continuous time: but the camera could only accommodate ten minutes' worth of film. The story begins at 7.30 p.m. and ends at 9.15 p.m. (105 minutes later). But the film comprises eight reels of ten minutes each (81 minutes) (with credits added); so, what happened to the missing 25 minutes? Do we experience the film as shorter than 105 minutes? No: it never seems shorter than it should and there's no sense of haste or editing; indeed, many people experience the film as being longer than its actual running time.

How can we account for this perceived time?

1. Most of the action takes place in the living room of a penthouse in summer, with the New York skyline visible through a

panoramic window. At the beginning, the light suggests late afternoon; by the end, it's dark. Our daily experience of fading daylight makes us perceive the real-time action as taking long enough to cover the several hours of approaching darkness; in fact, Hitchcock artificially accelerated these light changes.

2. Similarly, the nature and context of the depicted action trigger other automatic judgements about time. After the proverbial Hitchcock murder at the beginning of the first reel, the story focuses on an elegant dinner party hosted by the two murderers and attended by relatives and friends of the victim. The actual time during which food is served spans two reels (about 20 minutes), but viewers attribute more time to that sequence because we know that neither the hosts nor the guests – who look calm, polite, and unhurried – would get through dinner at such a fast pace. When the action later splits – some guests chat in the living room in front of the camera, while others retire to another room to look at rare books – we reasonably see this off-screen episode as lasting longer than the few minutes it actually takes.

3. There are no 'jump-cuts' within each ten-minute reel: the camera glides slowly toward and away from each character. Yet Hitchcock finished most takes with a close-up of an object as a way of joining different segments. In most cases, the camera moves to the back of an actor wearing a dark suit and the screen goes black very briefly; the next take begins as the camera pulls away from the actor's back. Although the black screen isn't meant to signal a time break, it may nonetheless contribute to the perception of time having passed: we're used to interpreting breaks in the continuity of visual perception as a break in the continuity of time. Film-editing techniques (such as the dissolve and fade) often lead us to infer that time has elapsed between the preceding and following shots. In *Rope*, each of the seven breaks delays real time by a fraction of a second – but cumulatively this may suggest that a longer period has passed.

4. When we're uncomfortable or worried, we often experience
    time as passing more slowly: we focus on negative images
    associated with our anxiety.[8] (see below). One researcher has
    shown that the brain generates images at faster rates when
    we're experiencing positive emotions (see below). He refers to
    his own experience of aircraft turbulence as 'achingly slow':
    his attention was directed towards the negative aspects of the
    situation. Perhaps the unpleasant nature of the murder at the
    centre of *Rope* conspires to stretch time in a similar way.[9]

By providing a significant discrepancy between real/objective time
and the audience's perception of time (mind time), *Rope* illustrates
how the experience of duration is a *construct*.[10] (See Chapter 1.)

THE EFFECTS OF BRAIN CHEMICALS ON THE JUDGEMENT OF TIME

As we noted at the end of Chapter 3, the *interval timer* (IT) operates
like a 'stopwatch' in the brain. According to *interval-timing theory*,
bursts of the neurotransmitter *dopamine* play an important role in
framing a time interval.[11] If this theory is correct, then diseases and
drugs that affect dopamine levels should also disrupt the IT mechanism. This is what some researchers have found.[12] (See Box 4.1.)

Box 4.1   The effect of neurotransmitters and hormones on the interval timer

- Patients with untreated Parkinson's disease release less
  dopamine into the striatum, causing their internal clock
  to run slow: they consistently *underestimate* the duration of
  time intervals.[13] If you ask most people to say (starting at
  a particular moment) when they think a minute has
  elapsed, their answer, typically, will be to say 'now' after
  35–40 seconds. Untreated Parkinson's patients are likely
  to choose a *longer* duration.[14]

- Marijuana also lowers dopamine levels and slows down time; by contrast, recreational stimulants (such as cocaine and methamphetamine) increase the availability of dopamine, making the IT speed up: time seems to *expand*.
- Adrenaline — and other stress hormones — also make the clock speed up: a second can feel like an hour during stressful situations;[15] see text below).

THE EFFECTS OF BRAIN DAMAGE AND DISEASE ON MIND TIME

Distortions in the judgement of time can also occur as a result of brain damage and disease.

One demonstration of this involves a 66-year-old man, who found one day as he drove to work that other traffic seemed to be rushing towards him at terrific speed; he simultaneously felt that his own car seemed to be going unusually fast. Even when he slowed down to walking pace, it seemed to be hurtling along beyond his ability to control it. Also, he couldn't watch television: things happened too quickly for him to keep up with the storyline. When given the '60-second test' (to indicate when a minute had passed), it took almost five minutes for him to say 'now'. Doctors discovered a growth in his prefrontal cortex.[16]

Damage to the basal ganglia and/or frontal lobes sometimes produces *catatonia*: the patient may become 'frozen', like a living statue, 'caught' in mid-action with their hand outstretched as though reaching for something, or contorted into strange postures for days at a time (which would normally produce extreme discomfort). Although they don't seem to be conscious during these episodes, some patients have later reported that they could remember it; however, their recollections lacked any sense of passing time: their consciousness was completely still and devoid of possibilities. A sense of timelessness — though markedly *full* of possibility — is also reported by people in meditation or trance.[17]

AMNESIA AND MIND TIME

Some of the most dramatic – and extreme – case studies of mind-time distortion involve damage that has occurred to the patient's memory. People who sustain damage to regions of the brain involved in learning and recalling new facts develop major disturbances in their ability to place past events in the correct era and sequence. These *amnesics* also lose the ability to estimate the passage of time accurately at the scale of hours, months, years, and decades; this occurs despite their biological clock often remaining intact, and being able to judge brief intervals (a minute or less) and to order them correctly. At the very least, the experience of these patients suggests that the processing of time and certain types of memory must share some common neurological pathways.

The association between amnesia and time can be seen most dramatically in cases of permanent brain damage to the hippocampus, a region that's crucial to memory, and to the nearby temporal lobe, through which the hippocampus holds a two-way communication with the rest of the cortex.

Damage to the hippocampus prevents the creation of new memories (*anterograde amnesia*). The ability to form memories is an indispensable part of the construction of a sense of our own chronology: we build our *time line* event by event, connecting personal happenings to those that occur around us. An impaired hippocampus makes it impossible to hold factual memories for longer than about one minute; a dramatic case of the effects of hippocampal damage is that of Clive Wearing, which is described in Box 4.2.

Box 4.2   Clive Wearing

- Clive Wearing was the chorus master of the London Sinfonietta and a world expert on Renaissance music, as well as a BBC radio producer. In March 1985, he suffered a rare brain infection caused by the cold sore virus (*Herpes simplex*). The virus attacked and destroyed his hippocampus, as well as parts of his cortex.

- He lives in a snapshot of time, constantly believing that he's just awoken from years of unconsciousness. For example, when his wife, Deborah, enters his hospital room for the third time in a single morning, he embraces her as if they'd been separated for years, saying "I'm conscious for the first time" and "It's the first time I've seen anybody at all".

- At first, his confusion was total and very frightening to him. Once, he held a chocolate in the palm of one hand and covered it with the other for a few seconds until its image disappeared from his memory. When he uncovered it, he thought he'd performed a magic trick, conjuring the chocolate from nowhere. He repeated it over and over, with total astonishment and increasing fear each time.

- He can still speak and walk, read music, play the organ and conduct; in fact, his musical ability is remarkably well-preserved. He can learn new skills (such as mirror-reading), which he performed just as well after three months. Yet for Clive, it's new every time.

- His capacity for remembering his earlier life is extremely patchy. For example, when shown pictures of Cambridge (where he'd spent four years as an undergraduate and had often visited subsequently), he only recognized King's College chapel – the most distinctive Cambridge building – but not his own college. He couldn't remember who wrote Romeo and Juliet, and he thought Queen Elizabeth and Philip, Duke of Edinburgh (both then still alive) were singers he'd known from a Catholic church.

- According to Deborah, 'without consciousness he's in many senses dead'. In his own words, his life is 'Hell on earth – it's like being dead – all the bloody time'.

- This illustrates dramatically a *loss of time awareness*, showing how fundamental memory – in particular, *episodic memory* (EM) [18] – is to our sense of identity and our ability to function in society. [19] (See Box 4.5.)

The memories that the hippocampus helps to create aren't actually stored there: they're distributed in neural networks located in parts of the cortex (including the temporal lobe) related to the material being recorded (areas dedicated to vision, sound, touch, etc.). These networks must be activated to both lay down and recall a memory: when they're destroyed, patients cannot recover long-term memories (*retrograde amnesia*). The memories most markedly lost in retrograde amnesia are precisely those that bear a *time stamp*: recollections of unique, personal events that occurred in a particular context on a particular occasion (i.e. *episodic memory*). The temporal lobe, which surrounds the hippocampus, is critical in making and retrieving such memories.

In patients with *temporal lobe damage* (as a result of viral encephalitis, stroke, or Alzheimer's disease), years and even decades of autobiographical memory can be permanently destroyed. A patient, who, at the age of 46, sustained damage both to the hippocampus and to parts of the temporal lobe resulted in *both* anterograde and retrograde amnesia. Like Clive Wearing, he inhabits a permanent present, unable to remember what happened a minute or 20 years ago. Indeed, he has no sense of time at all: he's unable to state the date or his age (guessing as wildly as 1943 and 2013). Without a watch or window (that provides light and shadow clues), morning is no different from afternoon, or night from day: the body clock doesn't help (see Chapter 3). He knows he was married (but his wife divorced him more than 20 years previously) and has two children (he's actually a grandfather), but he cannot place himself in the time line of his family life.[20]

MENTAL DISORDER AND MIND TIME

One demonstration of the 'time discontinuity phenomenon' in relation to 'model psychosis experiments' involved the hallucinogenic drug mescaline.[21] In one such experiment, the participant (the researcher himself) played chess with the experimenter (with whom he'd previously played). He experienced a number of paranoid delusions that focused on the taking of his chess pieces. Despite acknowledging that he'd taken a substantial amount of mescaline as part of a scientific experiment, and having no reason to believe that his opponent would have cheated, and despite having absolutely no memory of his pieces having been taken during the course of the game, this was the only explanation McKellar could come up with for how he'd lost his pieces.[22]

Interviews with several psychotic patients with persecutory delusions provided evidence of similar experiences of time discontinuity. Blank periods – periods of brief amnesia – can occur, but events do happen within them of which the patients have no awareness. The result can be alarming impressions of objects and people appearing and disappearing unpredictably, rather than moving about in the way we're used to seeing them with normal and continuous passage of time. (This is similar to Clive Wearing's 'chocolate experience': see Box 4.2.)

Such uncaused, unexplained, often frightening unexpected events can provide the content for delusions, including those in which these events are seen as resulting from the activities of one's 'persecutors'.[23]

Such paranoid delusions are a common feature of schizophrenia (and other forms of psychosis), the most serious form of mental disorder. Could they reflect a faulty internal clock? Or might it work the other way? Schizophrenia certainly seems to affect people's perception of time. If someone with schizophrenia is shown a flash of light and presented with a sound separated by one-tenth of a second, they typically have trouble saying which came first; they also estimate the passing of time less accurately than those without schizophrenia.[24]

Several studies have shown that if you disturb the internal clocks of healthy people, you can create some of the symptoms associated with schizophrenia, including delusions. In one experiment, healthy participants learned to play a video game in which they had to steer a plane around obstacles; once they'd got used to the game, the researchers inserted a 0.2-second delay in the plane's response to movements of the mouse. Initially, performance worsened, but participants eventually adjusted to the delay: mouse movements and plane movements were now perceived as simultaneous. However, when the researchers removed the delay, the participants now experienced the plane to be moving *before* they consciously steered it with the mouse.[25]

This is remarkably similar to how people with schizophrenia describe feelings that they're somehow being controlled by another being. There's also some evidence that 'schizophrenic brains' are temporally inflexible: using a video game similar to the steering a plane game, it was found that people with schizophrenia (compared with healthy controls) find it more difficult to compensate for delays between their actions and the outcomes of their actions.[26] During a broad range of mental tasks, people with schizophrenia display less activity in their cerebellum.[27]

Box 4.3 The tickle test

- Try tickling yourself.
- Does it work – can you make yourself laugh?
- If not, try explaining this in terms of the timing of the stimulus (the tickling movements) and the response (laughing)?
- How might the timing relationship be changed in order to make it work?

We cannot normally tickle ourselves: somehow, the intention to make the necessary movements also suppresses the response. But in one experiment, participants were asked to brush the palm of their hand using a robotic probe which produced a 200-millisecond delay between the intended movements and the actual movements; under these conditions, participants experienced the same sensations as they would have if someone else did the tickling.[28]

In fact, voice-hearing psychotic patients display a greater ability to tickle themselves compared with non-psychotic controls.[29] Could it be that for people with schizophrenia there's some kind of delay between intention and response? Might poor time-processing explain many of the schizophrenic person's experience? For example, by muddling the order of thoughts and perceptions within your brain, you might move your hand before becoming conscious of the decision, making it feel as if someone else is controlling your movements. Again, when an ad. appears on television, your brain might picture the product before you consciously register seeing it on the screen; this could create the disturbing illusion that your thoughts are being broadcast on television.[30]

In relation to auditory-verbal hallucinations, some researchers have attempted to directly measure *source monitoring* – the capacity to distinguish between self-generated thoughts and externally presented stimuli. One idea is that hallucinating patients have *dysfunctional metacognitive beliefs* (beliefs about their own mental processes) that lead them to make self-defeating efforts to control their thoughts; this makes the thoughts seem unintended – therefore, alien. A second idea is that source monitoring errors reflect a general failure to monitor one's own intentional states: hallucinating patients don't display the same dampening in the auditory perception areas of the temporal lobe seen during talking and inner speech (internal thought).[31]

Perhaps the most extreme example of a mental disorder that involves a distortion of mind time is Cotard's syndrome. This is an uncommon condition in which the central feature is a *nihilistic delusion*; in its complete form, this leads the patient to deny his or her own existence and that of the external world.[32] There have been several different interpretations of this delusion, including those deriving from Freud's psychoanalytic theory; one such is the claim that the fundamental disturbance involved is an 'abnormal intuition of subjective time'.[33]

Another interpretation focuses on a persistent, deep sense of guilt, which may engender self-punishment, with a desire to sever contact with all human relations in a world in which the existence of space and time is completely denied. Commonly, Cotard's patients come to believe that not only are they dead but also immortal: this means they will remain in their 'I am dead' state forever, with no possibility of release through death, in effect, a state of 'everlasting death' and hence everlasting despair.[34]

Mental time lag and consciousness

While most of us don't have to grapple with the large gaps of memory or the chronological confusion experienced by Clive Wearing, we do all share a strange mental time lag, a phenomenon first identified by the neurophysiologist, Benjamin Libet. His research is described in Box 4.4.

Box 4.4   Libet's experiments on consciousness and free will

- Libet asked the question: when someone spontaneously and deliberately flexes his/her finger or wrist, what starts the action off? Is it the conscious decision to act, or is it some unconscious brain process?[35]
- To find out, Libet asked participants to flex their finger/ wrist at least 40 times, at times of their own choosing, and measured the following:
  1. The time at which the action occurred (M); this was detected by using electrodes on the wrist (*electromyo-gram/EMG*).
  2. The beginning of brain activity in the motor cortex; this was detected via electrodes on the scalp (*electro-encephalogram/EEG*), which can detect a gradually increasing signal called the *readiness potential/RP*.
  3. The time at which the participant consciously decided to act (the *moment of willing/W*). Libet devised a special method for measuring this: participants

---

were asked to note the position of a spot of light that moved around the circumference of a circular screen *at the moment they decided to act*. They could then say, after the action had occurred, where the spot had been at that critical moment.

The key question (as far as the issue of free will is concerned) is: which of these comes first?

Libet found that W came about 200 milliseconds (ms) (one-fifth of a second) *before* the action (consistent with the concept of free will). But the RP began about 300–500 ms *before that* (500–700 ms *before the action* – contrary to what belief in free will would predict). So, there was brain activity for anything up to *half a second* before participants were subjectively aware of having made the decision to act: *consciousness lagged behind brain activity*.

Libet's results caused a storm of debate among philosophers, neuroscientists, psychologists, and physiologists, which has been raging ever since.[36] What was controversial was the blow they appeared to deal to our cherished belief in free will.[37]

There are two further questions raised by Libet's findings: (1) why aren't we aware of this delay between brain activity and consciousness? (2) how should we view or experience the present, the 'now'?

1. One attractive explanation of why we're unaware of the delay is that because we have similar brains that work in similar ways, we're all 'hopelessly late for consciousness' and no one notices it. But perhaps more likely is that the brain can institute its own connections on the central processing of events, such that, at the microtemporal level, it manages to 'antedate' (predate) some events so that delayed processes can appear less delayed, and differently – delayed processes can appear to have similar delays.[38] This possibility may explain why we maintain the illusion of continuity of time and space when we move our eyes more quickly from one target to another: we notice neither the

blur that accompanies the eye movements, nor the time it takes to move the eyes from one place to another. One suggestion is that the brain predates the perception of the target by as much as 120 ms, thereby giving us all the *illusion* of seamless viewing.[39]

> The brain's ability to edit our visual experience and to impart a sense of volition after neurons have already acted is an indication of its exquisite sensitivity to time ...'[40]

2. The delay – of up to half a second – in the appearance of awareness of a sensory event introduced a problem regarding how to define or understand 'the present moment'.[41] However, the brain's ability to 'predate' some events (subjective referral backward in time: Libet) puts the *subjective* experience of the present back into the present: actual awareness of the present is really delayed, but the *content* of the conscious experience is brought into alignment with the present. So, *subjectively*, we do live in the antedated present, although in fact we're not aware of the present for up to half a second after the sensory signal arrives at the cerebral cortex.[42]

According to the philosopher, Ludwig Wittgenstein, 'The present is neither past or future. To experience the present is therefore a phenomenon with timelessness'.[43] But if our experience of a sensory stimulus is actually antedated after the half-second delay, the experience is actually one of an event a half-second in *the past*: as the subjective present is actually of a past sensory event, it cannot be 'timeless'.[44]

TIME EXPANSION EXPERIENCES (TEEs): THE SLOWING DOWN OF TIME

As commonly portrayed in television and film, someone facing a frightening, potentially dangerous or even fatal situation – such as losing control of a car and heading for another vehicle or the edge of a cliff – experience a dramatic slowing down of time: things seem to happen in *slow motion*.

Neuropsychologist David Eagleman experienced this apparent slowing down of time as an eight-year-old when he fell off a roof and broke his nose. This phenomenon could either be related to memory, or it could be that the brain's processing speed *accelerates* under stressful conditions, making external events appear to slow down in comparison. Eagleman decided to replicate his childhood experience under carefully controlled conditions.

With his colleagues, Eagleman asked six Psychology graduate students to take a thrill ride known as a 'suspended catch air device'; this drops people from a 31 metre (150 feet) scaffolding tower into a safety net below.[45]

To measure the speed of their perceptions, the participants wore a specially designed wrist-worn device (a perceptual chronometer). An LED array on the face of the device displayed as a flickering single-digit number alternating with the negative of its image about 20 times per second; this is normally too fast for people to distinguish between the two images (you'd just perceive all the elements of the LED array as shining simultaneously). However, if the perceptual clocks of the terrified participants speeded up just a little, the number should become visible.

As predicted, they *overestimated* the time it took to drop into the net (they estimated over three seconds, compared with the actual 2.5 seconds). However, contrary to predictions, the participants couldn't identify the flickering number on the display (suggesting that their perceptions *hadn't* actually speeded up). Eagleman seems to have shown that time itself doesn't actually slow down when we're afraid, and nor does the brain's sensory processing speed up. What changes is our *perception* of time.

These experiences in which time appears to slow down and expand have been called *Time Expansion Experiences* (TEEs).[46] In a collection of 74 reports of TEEs, 40 were linked to accidents (mostly involving cars), 12 to meditation or spiritual experiences, seven to sport and games, and a further seven to psychedelic drugs. Their main features are described in Box 4.5.

Box 4.5   The major features of TEEs[47]

- Most participants described their TEEs as positive, even if they occurred in accidents and emergencies.
- Almost everyone reported a sense of calmness, despite the danger they were (in most cases) facing.
- Most also reported a sense of alertness or even heightened awareness, rapid and detailed thinking: their slowed down sense of time provided an opportunity to formulate plans, make decisions, and take preventative action.
- Some reported a sense of quietness, as if the usual noise around them had become muffled.
- In many cases, the time expansion was very dramatic: seconds seemed like minutes – or time seemed to stop or disappear altogether.

So how does this happen?

Explaining TEEs

The apparent slowing down of time is attributable to a trick of memory. An intense experience involving increased fear or excitement focuses our attention and produces the firing of many neurons across the brain; this causes us to absorb more sensory information. Richer memories seem to last longer, because we assume that more time would have been needed to record so many details.[48]

This could account for other temporal illusions, such as the 'oddball effect'. When participants see the same things repeatedly (such as the image of a dog flashed on a computer screen) and then suddenly see something different (say, an image of Margaret Thatcher), the novel stimulus seems to last longer – even if all the images are in fact presented for the same duration. Studies using fMRI (functional magnetic resonance imaging) show a spike in brain activity in response to an unexpected stimulus, suggesting that it causes a richer memory to be formed; in turn, this explains why the experience seems to last/have lasted longer. In a reframed version of this memory explanation, it has been proposed that the experience of duration is a 'signature' of the amount of energy expended in representing a stimulus (the coding efficiency).[49]

According to John Wearden, a British Experimental Psychologist, the massively increased pace of the internal clock during stressful events may have adaptive advantage: the perceived slowing down of external events may provide a valuable opportunity for flight-or-fight decisions to be made.[50] However, laboratory studies of the effect of arousal on subjective time haven't wholly supported this account: experimental manipulations designed to moderately increase physiological arousal have little or no effect on subjective time estimates. Wearden suggests that the relationship between subjective time and arousal may be non-linear: changes in the pace of the internal clock may only be seen at extreme levels of arousal (very high or very low), which are difficult to induce under laboratory conditions.

However, when participants were exposed to ten seconds of fast clicks (about five per second) and then asked to estimate the duration of a burst of light or a sound, they believed that the second stimulus lasted about ten per cent longer than if they'd heard silence or white noise before the burst.[51]

Had their central pacemaker actually speeded up, or could the results have simply been due to a distortion of memory? Participants' rate of mental processing was tested in a replication of the experiment described above.[52] After being exposed to a click, participants performed three different tasks: basic arithmetic, memorizing words, and hitting a specified key on a computer keyboard. What the researchers found was that the clicks accelerated performance on all three tasks by 10–20 per cent; white noise had no effect. According to Wearden, if you speed up people's subjective time, they really do seem to have more time to process things, and the practical implications are enormous (such as allowing students to cram more work into less time).

The fact that there was no evidence of changes in participants' heart rate, skin conductance (galvanic skin response/GSR), or muscle tension, suggests strongly that the results weren't merely the result of increased autonomic arousal (as claimed by some critics, including Eagleman). So, how else might the clicks be changing time perception and information-processing speeds?

Research has found that rhythmic sounds can entrain gamma brain waves: this causes the beginning of each sound to be accompanied by a burst of several especially strong wave peaks. The clicks may also entrain other types of brain waves, perhaps including those that correspond to the discrete snapshots in our perceptions. Faster oscillations produce more snapshots per second, making a given time period seem to last longer.[53] If this explanation is correct, the clicks are literally resetting the brain's *frame-capture rate*.[54]

According to William James, 'A day full of excitement is said to pass 'ere we know it'. On the contrary a day full of waiting, of unsatisfied desire for change, will seem a small eternity.[55] Corresponding to these two extremes – in the modern idiom, 'time flies when you're having fun' – or whenever we're exposed to new, fast-changing, complex stimuli (such as playing an exciting video game) – or time 'drags' when we're bored.

A recent, once-in-a-lifetime 'natural experiment' came in the form of the 2020 Covid-19 lockdown in many parts of the world. The study of a UK sample is described in Box 4.6.[56]

Box 4.6 How did lockdown affect the speed of the passing of time?

- A total of 604 people were recruited online (via email or social media advertising) between April 7 and 30, 2020, having experienced between 14 and 38 days of lockdown when completing questionnaires that assessed affect (emotional state), task load, stress levels, and level of satisfaction with their social interaction.

- They were asked to rate the speed of the passage of time per day and/or per week (depending on how long they'd been in lockdown when responding.
- Over 80 per cent experienced a distortion of time perception compared with their pre-lockdown perception.
- *Slowing* of perceived time per day was associated with increasing age (over 60) and stress, reduced task load, and reduced satisfaction with current levels of social interaction.
- *Slowing* of perceived time per week was associated with increasing age and reduced satisfaction with current levels of social interaction.
- *Speeding up* of perceived time (per day) was associated with decreasing age (under 60), and increased satisfaction with current levels of social interaction, decreased stress levels and increased task demands.

The changes in social and physical distancing imposed during lockdown had a significant effect on people's perception of the speed with which time passes. While some of these findings are consistent with James's claims (see above), others suggest that the situation is far more complex than James believed; while Ogden identified a small number of factors that impacted time perception, she acknowledges that there are several others whose influence her study didn't attempt to identify.[57]

TEEs as altered states of consciousness

Perhaps the best way of understanding dramatic TEEs is in relation to *altered states of consciousness* (ASC).[58]

Our experience of time is closely bound up with our sense of self and our state of consciousness. When we shift into a different state of consciousness, due to unusual circumstances or triggers, then we shift into a different 'timeworld' in which time expands dramatically.[59]

When we experience dramatic variations in our time perception, such as in accidents or emergencies, it's because we move out of our usual state of consciousness and into a dramatically altered state.

Another way of looking at these changes would be to think in terms of *a loss of the sense of self*. 'Inner time or duration is virtually indistinguishable from the awareness of the self, the experience of the self as an enduring, unitary entity that is constantly becoming'.[60] When accidents and emergencies occur, they bring about a shift into an ASC, due to their sheer shock and intensity: our usual sense of self can suddenly and dramatically change, along with our perception of time.[61]

Near-death experiences (NDEs) represent a quite extreme, dramatic example of ASC. NDEs were popularized by Moody, an American psychiatrist, in his book *Life after Life*.[62] Based on accounts of numerous survivors of cardiac arrest (CA) and other life-threatening situations, Moody presented a description that included:

i. experiences of floating along a dark tunnel with a bright light at the end;

ii. leaving the body and being able to watch the proceedings from above (an *out-of-body experience*/OBE);

iii. meeting a 'being of light' (a spiritual being and/or deceased loved ones) who helps the person review his/her past life;

iv. feeling as if s/he were passing into another world (the light), where some final barrier marked the return from joy, love, and peace, to pain, fear, or sickness; the person must choose between carrying on into the light and returning to life's pain and suffering.

While much of the debate and research into the nature of NDEs has focused on whether or not they provide evidence of life after death (the *survivalist* argument), more relevant here is another common feature, namely, the disparity between the experienced duration of the NDE and objective time. For example, people commonly report that their experience lasted for hours or even days – or even longer – when the time spent in CA, unconscious or even without displaying brain activity, may have been just seconds or minutes.[63]

This time disparity is particularly marked in the case of the life-review element ((iii) above): it's commonly claimed that the whole of an individual's life is replayed in a fraction of a second.[64]

An NDE *could* be experienced prior to the interval during which brain function ceases, such that upon regaining consciousness, the experient believes that it occurred just seconds prior to revival – *regardless* of how much time had passed in real (clock) time.[65] A person might even start having an NDE prior to the cessation of brain activity, which then might stop along with the loss of consciousness, but then resume where it left off when brain activity begins to function again;[66] in other words, the experient would have no awareness/memory of the time interval during which they lost consciousness, so that the NDE seems to be continuous, uninterrupted – and, often, long-lasting.

Speeding up and slowing down reversed

Presumably, in 'a day full of excitement' as James put it, our limited attentional resources are fully taken over by the demands of the fast-paced, changing stimulation.[67]

While there's certainly anecdotal evidence to support these views of time perception, in retrospect these relations can become *reversed*. For example, the enjoyable holiday that seemed to fly by at the time seems, when we look back on it, to have 'lasted an age'. By the same token, the succession of dull days, when time dragged, seems, on reflection, to have passed quite quickly.[68]

Experimental findings have been reported which support this anecdotal evidence.[69] One group of participants watched a nine-minute clip from the movie *Armageddon*; a second group spent the same amount of time in a waiting room doing nothing. As predicted – and consistent with James's observation – the first group reported that time passed much faster compared with the second group. However, when the participants were questioned some time later, the second group estimated the time they'd spent just waiting as ten per cent *shorter* than those who'd watched the movie.

What seems to be crucial is the *quantity of accumulated memory*: rich and varied memories (of the film) are associated with long periods, while less intense or similar memories are associated with shorter ones. This neatly illustrates that the subjective experience of time arises from the interplay – or perhaps the by-product – of attention and memory processes.[70]

DOES TIME REALLY GO FASTER AS WE GET OLDER?

We know that time has an impact on memory, but it is also memory that creates and shapes our experience of time. Our perception of the past moulds our experience of time in the present to a greater degree than we might realise. It is memory that creates the peculiar, elastic properties of time. It not only gives us the ability to conjure up a past experience at will, but to reflect on those thoughts through autonoetic consciousness – the sense that we have of ourselves as existing across time – allowing us to re-experience a situation mentally *and* to step outside those memories to consider their accuracy.[71]

As we shall see below, memory may also play a crucial role in the common observation that time speeds up as we age. *Why Life Speeds Up As You Get Older* is the title of a book by Dutch Psychologist, Douwe Draaisma; its subtitle is *How Memory Shapes Our Past*, and the major kind of memory in question is *autobiographical* memory (AM).[72]

As we noted in Box 4.2, Clive Wearing's capacity for remembering major features of his past, including his knowledge of 'current affairs', was almost totally destroyed along with destruction of his hippocampus. However, other abilities were well-preserved, as was his ability to acquire new skills (although he couldn't recall that he'd acquired them). These apparent contradictions within his long-term memory (LTM) illustrate crucial distinctions between *episodic memory* (EM), *semantic memory* (SM),[73] and *procedural memory* (PM);[74] these distinctions overlap with that between *declarative memory* (DM) and PM.[75] (See Box 4.7.)

Box 4.7 Different kinds of long-term memory

- *Declarative memory* (DM) (or 'knowing that') embraces both *episodic memory* (EM) (e.g. 'I started piano lessons when I was seven') and *semantic memory* (SM) (e.g. 'I know the difference between a major and a minor key').

- *Procedural memory* (PM), is 'knowing how' (e.g. 'I know how to play *Moonlight Sonata*).

- EM is a form of 'autobiographical' memory, responsible for storing a record of our past experiences – the events, people, objects, etc. which we've personally encountered. It usually includes details regarding the particular time and place in which events and other people were experienced (they have a *spatio-temporal context*), as in 'What did you do last night?' EMs also have a *subjective* (self-focused) reality, but most could, in principle, be verified by others.

- *Flashbulb memories* are a special kind of EM: we can give vivid and detailed accounts of where we were and what we were doing when we first heard about some major national or international event.[76]

- *Semantic memory* (SM) refers to our store of general, factual knowledge about the world, including concepts, rules, and language, 'a mental thesaurus'.[77] SM doesn't itself refer to where and when that knowledge was originally acquired. For example, we don't remember 'learning to talk' – we just 'know English' (or whatever our native language happens to be). However, SM can also store personal information (such as how many siblings we have, or where we were born).

- Procedural memory (PM) refers to information from LTM which cannot be inspected consciously. For example, playing the piano is a complex skill which is also very difficult to describe; trying to explain how to tie a shoelace is even harder than the skill itself. In the same way, native speakers of a language cannot usually describe the complex grammatical rules that govern 'correct use of that language' – perhaps because they weren't learned consciously in the first place. By contrast, both EM and SM can be inspected consciously, and their content can be described to another person.

'Our memory has a will of its own';[78] similarly, memory has been likened to a dog that lies down where it pleases. Our autobiographical memory (AM):[79]

... is the chronicle of our lives, a long record we consult whenever someone asks us what our earliest memory is, what the house we lived in as a child looked like, or what was the last book we read. Autobiographical memory recalls and forgets at the same time ...[80]

AM obeys some mysterious laws of its own:

... Why does it contain next to nothing about what happened before we were three or four? Why are hurtful events invariably recorded in indelible ink? Why are humiliations remembered for years on end with the precision of a charge sheet? Why is it invariably set in motion at sombre moments and during sombre events? ... Now and then we are taken by surprise by our own memory. A smell suddenly reminds us of something we haven't thought about for thirty years ... Memories of youth can seem clearer in old age than they were at the age of forty ...[81]

EXPLAINING THE SPEEDING UP OF TIME AS WE GET OLDER

Draaisma discusses three such explanations: (i) telescopy; (ii) reminiscence; and (iii) physiological changes.

The telescopy phenomenon

In 1955, Gray, an American statistician, identified a pattern in how people respond to items in questionnaires. For example, in response to questions such as, 'How often have you visited your general practitioner during the past two years?', participants tended to overestimate the frequency when their answers were checked; they included visits that fell just outside the two-year period. So, people in general tend to date events *more recently* than they actually occur (the *telescopy phenomenon* (TP)/*forward telescoping*). It is as if time had been compressed and, as when looking through a telescope, things seem closer than they really are. The opposite is called backward/ reverse telescoping (also known as *expansion*): you guess that events occurred *longer ago* than they actually did; this is rare for distant events but not uncommon for recent weeks.[82]

The TP is highlighted under certain conditions. According to one early theory, time is based upon the basic analogy of *space* – not the geometric kind, but that used in perspective (i.e. space as manifested to the observer).[83] The experience of time involves 'internal optics: memory orders experiences in time much like a painter orders space with the use of perspective'. Memories lend depth to consciousness: as soon as the order in our memory is broken, as happens during the imperceptible transitions between brain images, our sense of time also disappears (see Chapter 1).

A number of factors influence the internal optics of mind time, including the intensity of our sensations and ideas, their alternation, number, and the tempo with which they succeed one another, how much attention we pay them, the effort needed to store them in memory, and the emotions and associations they conjure up in us. However, these very same factors that can help us find our bearings in time can also lead to mistaken estimates. For example, focusing our attention works like a telescope: the detail this reveals produces the illusion that the object is close to us – far closer than it really is. This analogy was borrowed from the English Psychologist, Sully, who observed that a sensational event – such as an abduction or murder – is estimated as being much more recent than it actually was.[84]

Although not mentioned by any of the early researchers, *age* can be added to the list of variables thought to contribute to the TP, and, in turn, to the explanation of the anecdotally common experience that time speeds up as we get older. While acknowledging that the subjective acceleration of time with age has been observed so often that it's probably true, it wouldn't be reflected in objective time judgements.[85] Both *age and gender* have been thought to affect the ability to date public events.[86]

When personally-significant incidents are involved (as in 'true' EM), it's often difficult to judge the extent of telescopy accurately; this problem is avoided when public events are involved (closer perhaps to flashbulb memories than EM in general.

The study (often referred to as the 'Margaret Thatcher study' investigated memory for public events over a seven-year period (1990–1996), comparing three age groups (18 – 21; 35–50; 60 and over). In the second part of the study, the two older groups were tested with events occurring between 1977 and 1989 to see if the effects of age became apparent only with longer retention periods.

The researchers found a tendency towards forward telescoping in the youngest group when dating recent events, but this tendency lessened with increasing age. With less recent events, although the middle group showed evidence of telescopy, the over-60s (average age about 70) now dated *too distantly*; it was as if they had turned the telescope around, thereby extending the interval.[88] While one study had found females to be more accurate daters (albeit when personal events were involved),[89] there was no such evidence of a gender difference of any kind.

With regard to the original hypothesis, the results indicated that older people really do believe that more time has passed than is the case, which is why the years seem to 'fly by as we get older':[90] time in the subjectively longer period must have passed more swiftly. However, it's very difficult to interpret the results of time perception research: a case can be made for drawing the *opposite* conclusion: namely, that it's precisely those who think something happened three years ago – when in fact it was five – who will claim that time flies:[91]

> ... [this] theory can only be saved by the assumption of a *reverse connection* between the overestimate of the duration of a period of time and its subjective tempo. That does indeed manifest itself with the quickened pace of a week on holiday, which upon one's return home seems longer than an ordinary week. However, in that case, both telescopy and reverse telescopy will make us feel that time is rushing past, and that robs them of any explanatory value.[92]

The most straightforward explanation of the TP is the *clarity of memory hypothesis*:[93] because we know that memories fade over time, we use the clarity of a memory as a guide to its recency. So, if a memory seems unclear, we infer that the event took place longer ago;[94] by the same token, we might assume that the more we know about a particular news event – national/international – the better able we would be to correctly date it. However, the 'Margaret Thatcher study' found no supporting evidence.[95]

Their British sample found it easiest to date a–f (correct month and year) (see Box 4.8). Surprisingly, how much participants knew about an event only made a difference to the accuracy of dating *if it happened before they were born*; for events that took place within their lifetime, they didn't appear to use knowledge to date them. Instead – unless we've not even heard of the event – we rely on memory; in such cases (of complete unfamiliarity), we tend to assume that it must have happened a *very* long time ago.[96]

Box 4.8 The effects of ageing on the dating of public events[87]

Try to identify the year in which each of the events listed below occurred:

a. The Chernobyl disaster *
b. The Lockerbie disaster *
c. Margaret Thatcher becoming British Prime Minister *
d. The Argentine occupation of the Falkland Islands *
e. The murder of John Lennon *
f. The assassination of Indira Gandhi *
g. The Harrods bombing *
h. The bombing of the Grand Hotel in Brighton *
i. The Silver Jubilee of Queen Elizabeth II *
j. The fall of the Berlin Wall *
k. South of England hurricane
l. Death of Michael Jackson
m. Hurricane Katrina hits New Orleans
n. Barack Obama is inaugurated as U.S. President
o. Death of Diana, Princess of Wales
p. Terrorist attack on the London Underground

(a–j are a sample of events from the study and formed part of a longer list; h–p are added to make the list of events more relevant to a wider age-range of readers.)

Answers can be found at the end of the chapter.

The reminiscence effect

As we noted above, telescopy is one of three accounts of the acceleration of the passing years: the other two are the *reminiscence effect* and *physiological clocks*. The first is described in Box 4.9.

Box 4.9   The reminiscence effect[97]

- Francis Galton, the English scientist (and cousin of Charles Darwin) identified what he called the *reminiscence bump*.[98]
- If older participants (60 and over) are given cue words to help them recall personal events (the 'Galton cueing technique'), there's an undeniable concentration of memories from an earlier age period covering some ten years, with age 20 lying at the centre.
- The bump increases further when the participant is asked to describe three or four of his/her most vivid memories: there's now a solid peak at age 15.
- The reminiscence effect (RE) becomes more prominent as age increases beyond 60.

One study used Galton's method to study the autobiographical memory of older participants (average age of 80), using cue words such as 'horse', 'river', and 'king'.[99] Most of the memories these words triggered stemmed from the first and (to, a somewhat lesser extent) second quarter of their lives. For most participants, the third quarter (age 40–60) showed a sharp drop. The same pattern, with small variations, has been found in dozens of other studies. Combining the findings of a long series of experiments, it has been concluded that the 'bump' is still absent in 40-year-olds, begins slowly in 50-year-olds, and becomes clearly visible among 60-year-olds.[100]

The RE is a robust phenomenon and is evident even in patients with Alzheimer's disease. Thirty healthy elderly participants and 30 Alzheimer's patients (aged 71–89) were given 15 minutes to relate their reminiscences of personally significant events. While the Alzheimer's patients recounted eight such events compared with the healthy group's 18, the distribution of their memories over the course of their life was similar: both groups had most to tell about their adolescence.[101]

How can we explain the RE?

Three accounts have been identified:[102]

1. Neurophysiologically, memory may be at its peak in our 20s, so that what we experience then is retained without difficulty; consequently, we store more memories then compared with any subsequent period. This explains why, 50 years later, the likelihood of retrieving memories from that time is so much greater. However, if the quality of a memory were its most important feature, then the reminiscence bump would have to occur some ten years earlier than studies usually show it does.

2. Between the ages of 15–25, we usually experience more that's worth remembering. This is suggested by the experimental finding that when participants are asked to recount three or four of their most vivid recollections, there's a stronger RE than when cue words are used. So, this explanation emphasizes the impact that the remembered event has made. As we might expect, these bump-related reminiscences are related to 'first times' of various types,[103] such as the first kiss, the first menstrual period, 'the first time', the first holiday without our parents, our first driving lesson, first day at work. Many of these have a 'flashbulb clarity' (see Box 4.7). While 'firsts' aren't exclusive to this early part of our life, they become decidedly less common as we get older.

3. During our youth and early adulthood, events occur that shape our personality, determine our identity, and guide the course of our life; these are the 'turning points' or 'formative experiences' that we tend to recall (and probably include one or more of the 'firsts' described above). The similarities between the present-day self and these formative experiences lead elderly people to remember those events almost automatically; they form part of our life history. Conversely, how we recount that history defines and demonstrates our identity. In old age,

people like to look back on their lives as a story that may hold surprises and unexpected changes, but which is nonetheless held together by the typical reactions of a stable central character. In the light of this stable self, much of what might at first have seemed new proves to be predictable, routine repetition and 'in character'.[104]

Whichever of these three explanations of the RE we consider the most valid (indeed, all three might contribute something to our understanding), several researchers have included the notion of *markers* in their accounts of time relationships in AM, including 'reference points'[105] and 'temporal landmarks';[106] these help determine how long ago we think some particular event took place (before or after the marker) and they may even help us determine the precise date on which the event occurred.

Only at moments when we're having real difficulty in dating a memory can we see our own time markers at work: they allow the memory to bounce between two ever-closer end-points.[107] The RE may be a consequence of the fact that a greater number of time markers become available for the period typically covered by it.[108] (See Box 4.8.)

A period that brings up many more memories will expand when seen in retrospect and seems to have lasted longer than an equally long period comprising few memories. Conversely, time markers will become less numerous at about middle age and later, and in the void thus created time will speed up subjectively ...[109]

This account has much in common with James's' view regarding the vivid and exciting memories of youth and the uniformity and routine of later years.[110] But in addition, the crucial factor might well be the *temporal organization* of memories:[111] if the network of time markers disappears (along with variety), then we've lost an important *access* to memories from that period.[112]

Physiological changes and the perception of time

This final explanation of the acceleration of time with age relates to *biological/body time* (see Chapter 3). One relevant finding concerns the *suprachiasmatic nucleus* (SCN): depletion of SCN cells and of dopamine production, both of which occur in old age, may cause crucial problems for how we deal with time. These physiological changes may underlie the results of experiments in which older people were asked to estimate how long it took for a three-minute interval to pass[113] (see pages 48–9).

Children's ability to estimate time accurately increases with age, peaking at around age 20; the ability of elderly people drops to the level of young children. Older people invariably *overestimate* lapsed time intervals. Three age groups (19–24; 45–50; 60–70) were asked to mark a three-minute interval by counting down the seconds: the youngest group was extremely accurate, overestimating, on average, by just three seconds, compared with 16 seconds for the middle group and 40 seconds for the oldest. This effect was even more marked when participants were asked to repeat the task, this time when engaged in a distracting task (average overestimation = 46, 63, and 106 seconds, respectively).[114]

DÉJÀ VU

Déjà vu (French for 'already seen') refers to the sense of having encountered a situation before, identical in every detail, even though we know that we haven't in fact done so. It has intrigued philosophers, poets, Psychologists, doctors and others for centuries. Different attempts at explaining *déjà vu* involve different interpretations of just what kind of phenomenon it is: is it essentially to do with memory, time perception, temporal organization, a confusion between dream content and perception of the external world, or a brain-related phenomenon?

One early explanation proposes that *déjà vu* is a memory of something that used to be (consciously) present in our mind, namely *dreams*. For example, as soon as the similarity between some dream content and the current situation is strong enough, our current experience activates associations with the dream; this produces the sense of familiarity.[115] This represents the *negative* of what Freud called the *day residue*, fragments from conscious, waking life that become incorporated into that night's dream[116] (see Chapter 1).

For many Psychologists, including some early researchers, this dream-related hypothesis was too sweeping. Couldn't it simply be that *déjà vu* happens when something in the present resembles what we've actually experienced in the past (after all, this is what the term conveys)? William James had repeatedly managed to trace the familiarity of his own *déjà vu* experiences back to genuine memories: if we concentrate hard enough, we can begin to identify the differences between the two, with the original memory becoming fuller and the feeling of familiarity receding.[117] While agreeing with James, the Swiss psychoanalyst Oskar Pfister disagreed as to how the pairing came about: for James, this happened more-or-less by chance, while Pfister claimed that it was *functional* (a form of *ego defence* that we use to help deal with stressful feelings and situations).[118]

A great deal of research has focused on the possible link between *déjà vu* and epilepsy, especially the pre-seizure *aura* of some temporal lobe patients, a 'dreamy state'[119] (see Chapter 3). During the aura, the patient hears strange noises or has a strange taste in the mouth; this can be accompanied by a sensation of being lifted up unexpectedly or of seeing familiar shapes being stretched into bizarre dimensions. Shortly before the seizure, the normal sense of time seems to vanish, the patient has the feeling of being outside reality, may have vivid hallucinations, and everything seems unusually familiar ('reminscence': what we'd now call *déjà vu*).

Although it's very difficult to locate precisely where in the brain the *déjà vu* experience originates, studies involving patients with epilepsy and brain tumours point to the hippocampus and parahippocampal gyrus in the *right* hemisphere.[120] While brain pathology could underlie *déjà vu* in such patients, this doesn't mean that all or most such experiences are caused by brain pathology.

Spontaneous misfiring of neurons (seizures) happens occasionally (comparable to hiccups or muscle cramp) and go unnoticed; if they occur in brain structures that process familiarity (such as the hippocampus), such a misfiring may create a feeling of intense familiarity apparently disconnected from our current experience.[121]

Another brain dysfunction that could possibly produce déjà vu involves a brief disruption in the normal course of neural information transmission. Information is normally transmitted from our sense organs to the higher brain centres in a rapid and reliably regular way. But should there be even a very brief delay along one of these neural pathways, this slight neural 'hiccup' could change our level of awareness – and we might misinterpret this as familiarity.[122]

If we now extend this possibility to two neural pathways, each carries duplicate messages but follows different routes to the final destination in the higher brain centres where they converge. If one pathway is delayed (even by milliseconds), this gap in the arrival of the two messages may make the later one appear to repeat the earlier one.[123] The brain usually merges these separate neural messages, but a small temporal gap creates the illusion of two separate experiences, producing déjà vu.

This temporal gap interpretation may also explain the sense of precognition that occasionally accompanies déjà vu. If you focus on the delayed message, then there is a feeling that this has happened before (déjà vu); but if you focus on the leading message, then it triggers a sense of 'I know what's going to happen next' (precognition). Recent advances in brain imaging and electrical brain-recording techniques may soon allow us to track small changes in the electrochemical activity of very small brain regions. Technology also exists which allows us to present visual and auditory information asynchronously to each hemisphere, providing an experimental laboratory analogue of the neural delay theory of déjà vu.[124]

Time perception, déjà vu, and existentialism

If you have seen the 1993 film Groundhog Day, starring Bill Murray, what do you consider the film to really be about? (See Box 4.10.)

Box 4.10 *Groundhog Day*: the ultimate *déjà vu*?

- Bill Murray plays Phil Connors, a cynical, world-weary TV weatherman who makes the annual trip to a rural Groundhog festival: according to legend, the behaviour of a small rodent, set free from a box, indicates how soon winter will end and spring begin.
- The day, as usual, is a nightmare for him, but the real ordeal begins the following morning.
- Connors wakes to discover that, for some inexplicable reason, it's Groundhog Day again! Everything happens *exactly* as it did the previous day – but only he seems to be aware of this.
- The next day it happens again, and the day after that, and the day after that and so on. Connors is trapped, forced to endure the worst day of his life over and over again.

The film works perfectly as an existential allegory.[125] The French existentialist novelist Albert Camus's *The Myth of Sisyphus* likens the human condition to the Sisyphus of Greek legend who was condemned by the gods to roll a huge rock up a hill, only to see it roll all the way down again, repeatedly, for all eternity.[126] If the Greek myth speaks of the futility of human labour and toil, then Connors must endlessly endure a ritual he finds pointless and unpleasant, unable to share his pain with anyone. It's the existentialist picture of life in a Godless universe.

The second part of the film documents Connors's attempts to meet the existential challenges he faces. He passes through three stages (as described by Sartre, arguably the most famous of the French existentialists). First, he's opportunistic, exploiting the advantages his situation affords him, such as financial gain, sexual encounters, and (other) physical pleasures; however, the realization that whatever he gains is automatically removed the next day plunges him into pessimism and despair. Connors makes various melodramatic attempts at self-destruction, but none can prevent him from waking fit and well the following day to experience the torture all over again. Finally, he faces up to the necessity of confronting the true nature of his existence, dealing with issues such as freedom, choice, and responsibility.

While this makes for a 'happy ending' (along with the inexplicable return to 'normality'), this a disappointing conclusion.[127] Camus concluded that we have to imagine Sisyphus as happy in his labours: values can be constructed and simple contentment found in the face of cosmic absurdity. The choice is either to give in to futility or to make the best of the less-than-perfect hand we've been dealt: '… However unsatisfying life may seem to one in the throes of existential despair, the prospect of death's oblivion usually makes it seem more palatable …'.[128]

For many years now, existential despair and awareness of our mortality have been at the core of existentialist philosophy (with Sartre and Camus key 20th century figures). More recently, a growing number of research Psychologists have started to bring experimental methods to bear on these same concerns that lie at the heart of the human condition. Their work is the subject of Chapter 6.

[Answers to dates of events in Box 4.6]

- The Chernobyl disaster (1986)
- The Lockerbie disaster (1988)
- Margaret Thatcher becoming British Prime Minister (1979)
- The Argentine occupation of the Falkland Islands (1982)
- The assassination of John Lennon (1982)
- The assassination of Indira Gandhi (1984)
- The Harrods Bomb (1983)
- The bombing of the Grand Hotel in Brighton (1984)
- Elizabeth II's Silver Jubilee (1977)
- The fall of the Berlin Wall (1989)

- The South of England hurricane (1987)
- Death of Michael Jackson (2009)
- Hurricane Katrina hits New Orleans (2005)
- Barack Obama inaugurated as U.S. President (2009)
- Death of Diana, Princess of Wales (1997)
- Terrorist attack on the London Underground (2005)

NOTES

1. Hammond (2012)
2. McKellar (1968)
3. Ibid.
4. Both of these methods are ways of examining the *perception of duration* (or *subjective duration*), as distinct from the judgement of the *passage of time* (see Chapter 1).
5. Damasio (2012)
6. Ibid.
7. Ibid.
8. Stetson et al. (2007)
9. Damasio *op cit.*
10. Ibid.
11. Matell & Meck (2000)
12. Wright (2012)
13. Carter (2006); Wright *op cit.*
14. Ibid.
15. Wright *op cit.*
16. Binofski & Block (1996)
17. Carter *op cit.*
18. Tulving (1972)
19. Corballis (2011)
20. Damasio *op cit*
21. McKellar (1957)
22. Ibid.
23. McKellar (1968)
24. Fox (2009)

25. Ibid.
26. Eagleman (cited in Fox op cit.)
27. Andreasen & Pierson (2008)
28. Fox op cit.
29. Blakemore et al. (2000)
30. Fox op cit.
31. Ford & Mathlon (2004)
32. Enoch & Ball (2001)
33. Saavedra (1968)
34. Enoch & Ball op cit.
35. Libet (1985, 2004), Liber et al., 1983)
36. Banks & Pockett (2007)
37. See Gross (2023)
38. Damasio op cit.
39. Yarrow et al. (2001)
40. Damasio op cit. (p. 47)
41. Libet (2004) op cit.
42. Ibid.
43. Wittgenstein (1953) cited in Libet op cit. (p. 88)
44. Libet op cit.
45. Stetson et al., op cit.
46. Taylor (2020)
47. Ibid.
48. Eagleman & Pariyadath (2009)
49. Eagleman & Pariyadath (2010)
50. Cavanagh (2000)
51. Wearden (cited in Fox op cit.)
52. Ogden & Jones (2009)
53. Edward Large (cited in Fox op cit.)
54. Fox op cit.
55. James (1890, p. 626)
56. Ogden (2020)
57. Ibid.
58. Taylor (2021, p. 36)
59. Wittman (2018)
60. Hartcollis (1983)

61. Taylor (2021) *op* cit.

62. Moody (1975)

63. King (2021)

64. (1996)

65. French (2005)

66. King *op* cit.

67. Koch (2020)

68. Wallisch (2008)

69. McKellar (1968) *op* cit.

70. Wearden (2005) cited in Wallisch *op* cit.

71. Wallisch *op* cit.

72. Hammond (p. 150) *op* cit.

73. Draaisma (2004)

74. Tulving (1972)

75. Tulving (1985)

76. Cohen & Squire (1980)

77. Brown & Kulik (1977)

78. Tulving (1972) *op* cit.

79. Draaisma *op* cit.

80. Nooteboom (1983) cited in Drassima *op* cit.

81. Draaisma (p. 1) *op* cit.

82. *Ibid.* (pp. 1–2)

83. Hammond *op* cit.

84. Jean-Marie Guyau (1890) cited in Draaisma *op* cit.

85. Sully (1881)

86. Fraisse (1964)

87. Crawley & Pring (2000)

88. *Ibid.*

89. Draaisma *op* cit.

90. Skowranski & Thompson (1990)

91. Crawley & Pring *op* cit.

92. Draaisma *op* cit.

93. *Ibid.* (p. 217)

94. Bradburn et al. (1987)

95. Hammond *op* cit.

96. Crawley & Pring *op* cit.

97. Hammond *op cit.*
98. Draaisma *op cit.*
99. Galton (1879)
100. McCormack (1979)
101. Rubin & Schulkind (1997)
102. Fromholt & Larsen (1992)
103. Draaisma *op cit.*
104. Jansari & Parkin (1996)
105. Fitzgerald (1992)
106. Conway (1990)
107. Shum (1998)
108. Draaisma *op cit.*
109. Shum *op cit.*
110. Draaisma (p. 219) *op cit.*
111. James *op cit.*
112. Draaisma *op cit.*
113. Mangan (1996)
114. *Ibid.*
115. Freud (1900)
116. James *op cit.*
117. Oskar Pfister (1930) cited in Draaisma *op cit.*
118. See Gross (2020)
119. Jackson (1888)
120. Brown (2004)
121. Spatt (2002)
122. Brown *op cit.*
123. Miller & Goodale (1997)
124. Brown *op cit.*
125. Coniam (2001)
126. Camus (1942/2005)
127. Coniam *op cit.*
128. *Ibid.*

5

CULTURE AND GENDER

SHAPERS OF TIME

WHAT IS CULTURE?

Culture has been defined in various ways, but one definition that has wide appeal is the distinction between *objective aspects* (roads, bridges, cooking pots, military weapons, musical symphonies, and poetry) and *subjective aspects* (beliefs, attitudes, norms, roles, and values).[1]

So, culture is part of the environment made by humans; but, in turn, culture helps to 'make' humans.

> In essence, humans have an *interactive* relationship with culture: we create and shape culture, and are in turn influenced by our own cultural products.[2]

Culture is a *human universal*: it defines us as much as walking upright and possessing a large and complex brain define us (our 'natural habitat').[3] But at the same time, just like language and other defining human attributes, there are wide differences between different cultures with regard to both the objective and subjective aspects. To the list of subjective aspects above, we can add *perception of time/time perspective*.

DOI: 10.4324/9781032696218-5

CULTURAL DIMENSIONS AND SYNDROMES

Time is elastic in many cultures, but snaps taut in others. Indeed, the way members of a culture perceive and use time reflects their society's priorities and even their own worldview.[4]

Four major *cultural dimensions* have been identified, along which different cultures can be compared; one of these is *individualism-collectivism*, which defines one's identity in terms of personal choices/ achievements, and characteristics of the collective groups we're attached to, respectively.[5]

In addition, four major *cultural syndromes* have been proposed: patterns of values, attitudes, beliefs, norms and behaviours that can be used to contrast different groups of cultures, including *cultural complexity*; *individualism-collectivism*; and *tight vs. loose cultures*.[6]

In relation to time, *complexity* and *individualism-collectivism* are the most relevant. The more complex the culture, the more people must attend to time; this is related to the number and diversity of *social roles* that members of that culture typically play as time has to be allocated appropriately. More industrialized and technologically advanced cultures, such as the US and Japan, tend to be more focused on time – and, hence, are more complex.

Broadly speaking, capitalist politico-economic systems are associated with *individualism*, while socialist societies are associated with *collectivism*. Individualist cultures also tend to be Western, while collectivist cultures tend to be non-Western, traditional, and often non-industrialized.

Is it possible to define culture *in terms of time*?

Time is what brings us together. It is also what sets us apart. In the broadest sense, to be social is to be synchronized and keep together in time. It is to be collectively *in sync* ... We do synchronize our times eating, worshipping, studying, commemorating, and celebrating. All can be viewed under the lens of orchestrated temporal coincidence of individuals within a group. Time and timing do determine social bonding and is a universal measure of social cohesion. However, such determination may vary markedly across human societies ...[7]

Complementing this view of the fundamental importance of timing and synchronization of individuals' and groups' behaviour:

Humans have evolved to be *supercooperators*: it occurs within communities of ants, hunting dogs, meerkats, and baboons, but never as intensively or frequently as in humans. It's central to everyday human life. Many other species focus co-operative behaviour on those who share their genes. However, 'humans co-operate with friends, collaborators, strangers, other species, and even enemies upon occasion':[8]

TIME AS MONEY

As we noted in Chapter 2 when discussing language and time, English-speaking cultures – which are also likely to be both individualist and complex – see time as a *commodity*, a precious resource which can be 'used', 'saved', 'bought', 'wasted', and which should be rationed and controlled through the use of schedules and appointments. In collectivist cultures, time is regarded as a limitless, 'elastic' resource, which enables individuals to meet their obligations to various members of the community to whom they are bound.[9]

Birth, a British anthropologist, examined time perception in Trinidad and showed how understanding of 'time is money' can differ within the same overall culture. The title of his book, *Any Time Is Trinidad Time: Social Meanings and Temporal Consciousness*, refers to a commonly used phrase to excuse lateness: if you have, say, a 6 p.m. meeting, people may show up at 6.45 or 7.00 and say "Any time is Trinidad time". But when it comes to business, that loose approach works only for those in positions of power: a boss can arrive late and use the "any time is Trinidad time" excuse, but 'the workers' are expected to be more punctual.[10]

Birth wanted to know how closely time and money are associated in Trinidad. Farmers, whose days are dictated by natural events (such as sunrise: see Chapter 3), didn't recognize that association, despite having satellite TV and being familiar with Western popular culture. However, tailors in the same areas were aware of such notions.

MONOCHRONIC TIME AND POLYCHRONIC TIME

Cultures differ with respect to whether they view time either monochronically or polychronically.[11]

1. A monochronic view sees time as a scarce resource which must be rationed and controlled through the use of schedules and appointments and through aiming to do just one thing at a time. Sometimes spare time or time spent waiting is seen as something that needs to be 'killed'. We'd expect this view to be widely held within many individualist cultures.[12]
2. A polychronic view sees the maintenance of harmonious relationships as of critical importance, so that time needs to be used flexibly in order that we do right by the various people to whom we have obligations. This view is likely to predominate within many collectivist cultures.[13]

While this model is highly plausible, there are other cultural dimensions/syndromes that are also likely to be relevant in relation to time. For example, the uncertainty avoidance dimension is most probably linked to the degree to which we plan our use of time carefully in advance; this refers to the focus on planning and stability as ways of dealing with life's uncertainties.[14]

An initial series of studies compared various aspects of time management in seven countries. They found significant correlations between (i) the accuracy of clocks in public places; (ii) the speed at which people walked down the street in large (mostly capital) cities in summer weather; and (iii) the speed at which a post office clerk completed the sale of a low-denomination postage stamp.[15] Using these three measures as components, the researchers constructed a 'Pace of Life' Index for 31 countries (see Box 5.1).[16]

Box 5.1 The pace of life in 31 countries

- The pace of life appears to be *fastest* in Northern and Western Europe (Switzerland, Ireland, Germany, Italy, England, Sweden, Austria, Netherlands), and Japan.
- *Moderate nations*: France, Poland, Czech Republic, Costa Rica, the US, Canada, Hong Kong, Taiwan, Singapore, and Korea.
- *Slow-moving nations*: Greece, Bulgaria, Romania, Jordan, Syria, Kenya, Indonesia, China, El Salvador, Brazil, and Mexico.
- There was a strong link between a country's economic affluence and its citizens' typical pace of life; however, it's not possible to infer that the former is the cause of the latter.
- Other features of existing social structure – including attitudes regarding time-keeping/punctuality – are likely to be influences on pace of life.[17] For example, one study reported that in Brazil someone who always arrived late for appointments was rated as more likeable, happy, and successful than someone who didn't, while in the US someone who was always early was more likely to be seen in this positive way.[18]

The report of a case study of meetings between US and Mexican businessmen provides some important insights into the importance of shared views of time.[19] Each had a stereotyped view of the other's – and their own – time orientation; these were basically accurate in terms of behaviour (arrival times for meeting and compliance with deadlines). Both groups agreed that the Mexicans were *polychronic* and that the Americans were *monochronic* ('machines' as the Mexicans put it). Despite this agreement, the two groups were unable to do business together until each had understood why the other group perceived them as they did and collective decisions had been reached as to how to manage time.

PAST, PRESENT, FUTURE

How time is understood/conceptualized also differs between cultures. The predominant Western (Eurocentric) concept of time is *linear*: it travels in a straight line from past, through present, to future and is measured objectively in discrete units (see Chapter 1). Non-Western (especially Eastern) cultures are more likely see time as a wheel in which past, present and future revolve endlessly. For example, in Indian philosophy, time has no beginning (or its beginning remains unknown, or is unknowable), no middle, and no end. Time in India is often viewed as a 'quiet, motionless ocean', or 'a vast expanse of sky. The only exceptions to this flexible construction are found in relation to *auspicious events/situations* (see below). Such events, because of their religious significance, are seldom left to chance: one seeks divine guidance in their planning and execution.[20]

Western ways of life have become predominantly goal- and future-oriented. Time-saving technological devices help to increase productivity and efficiency, but they fail to free up actual time to enjoy oneself.[21] The concept of 'time famine' refers to the lack of time and people's difficulty in finding an optimal balance in their use of time; for example, do emails save us time or do we spend time sending more of them, both necessary and unnecessary? More broadly, the debate regarding the 'work-life balance' concerns the priority that many people, especially men, devote to their work relative to their family and leisure activities.

Some cultures conflate time and space: the Australian Aborigines' concept of 'Dreamtime' encompasses both a creation myth and a means of finding their way around the bush. Aborigines believe that their ancestors crawled out of the earth during Dreamtime: they 'sang' the world into existence as they moved around, naming each feature of the landscape and every living thing and thereby creating them. Even today, an entity doesn't exist unless an Aborigine 'sings' it.[22]

Sardar,[23] a British Muslim author and critic, has written about time and Islamic cultures, particularly the fundamentalist Wahhabism sect. Muslims always 'carry the past with them': in Islam, time is a tapestry incorporating the past, present and future, and the past is ever-present. Sardar claims that the West has 'colonized' time by spreading the expectation that life should become better with the passing of time. If you colonize time, you also colonize the future; if you think of time as an arrow (as Western cultures do: see above), you think of the future as progress, going in only one direction. But different people may desire different futures.

In a study comparing the time perspectives of American and various Indian all-male samples, participants were asked to write short stories, starting with single sentences provided for them, such as 'L.B. is beginning his new job ...'. The stories were analyzed to determine whether the major theme referred to the future or the past (there was no separate coding for the present). While 62 per cent of the American stories were set in the future, the figure for the Indian samples varied from 8 per cent (Brahmins) and 16 per cent (Muslims) to 56 per cent (Parsees) and 58 per cent (Kshatriya Hindus).[24] These findings underline the heterogeneity of Indian culture, and warn against making hasty generalizations based on single ethnic groups from a given country.[25]

The term 'auspiciousness' ('suggesting success or good fortune') can be used to highlight cultural differences regarding how time is understood. In Western (secular) thinking, the notion of auspiciousness doesn't hold the same meaning as it does for Hindus, Muslims, and Jews all over the world. In the West, there are a few events which might be construed as being auspicious, such as Easter, Christmas, baptisms, christenings, church weddings, sacramental rites, and funerals.[26]

In Sanskrit, 'auspiciousness' is referred to as *shub*; in ordinary, everyday language auspiciousness also refers to time and temporal events.[27] For Hindus, there is an auspicious time for most activities: starting a journey, travelling, going on a pilgrimage, starting a new business, buying a new house, moving into the house, time of birth, marriage, burial, cremation, and other activities. Auspiciousness is also associated with places, objects, or persons.

SPACE, TIME, AND LANGUAGE

Speakers of Kuuk Thaayorre (in Pormpuraaw, a small Aboriginal community in northern Australia) don't use relative spatial terms such as left and right. Rather, they talk in terms of absolute *cardinal directions* (north, south, east, west, and so on), and these are used at all scales/distances (for example, 'the cup is southeast of the plate'; or 'the boy standing to the south of Mary is my brother'). In Pormpuraaw, one must always stay oriented, just to be able to speak properly![27]

People who think differently about space are also likely to think differently about time. For example, researchers gave Kuuk Thaayorre speakers sets of pictures that showed *temporal progression*: a man ageing, a crocodile growing, a banana being eaten. They were then asked to arrange the shuffled pictures on the ground to indicate the correct temporal order. Each participant was tested twice, each time facing in a different cardinal direction. English speakers given this task will arrange the pictures so that time proceeds from left to right; Hebrew speakers (used to reading and writing from right to left) will tend to lay the pictures from right to left. This shows that reading/writing direction influences how we organize time. However, the Kuuk Thaayorre speakers didn't routinely arrange the pictures in any particular left/right or right/left way: instead, they arranged the pictures from *east to west*. When they were seated facing south, the cards went from left to right; when they faced north, they went from right to left. When they faced east, the pictures came towards the body, and so on. The researchers never told anyone which direction they were facing: the Kuuk Thaayorre knew that already and spontaneously used this spatial orientation to construct their representation of time.[28]

One study found that English speakers unconsciously sway their bodies *forwards* when thinking about the future and *backwards* when thinking about the past.[29] But in Aymara, a language spoken in the Andes of South America, the past is said to be in front and the future behind: the Aymara speakers' body language matches their way of talking.[30]

GENDER AND TIME

THE MENSTRUAL CYCLE

While it's highly likely that male and female members of a particular culture share a common view of time, it's equally likely that their respective *experience* of time is different.

As noted in Chapter 3, bodily/biological rhythms that have a cycle longer than 24 hours are called *infradian rhythms* and include the human menstrual cycle. The menstrual cycle is part of a broader picture of biological events which, like all biological events, both influence, and are influenced by, individual experience and patterns of social interaction (including attitudes, expectations, and related stereotypes). Traditionally, at least in Western countries, menstruation has had something of a taboo status: it's something to be kept completely private and never talked about in mixed company. Women themselves have both contributed to, and been victims of, the prejudiced view of menstruation as something unclean and to be ashamed of ('the woman's curse').

More recently, with advertising' of 'period products' on TV and elsewhere, and discussion of menstruation-related issues in the media (including the decision by women footballers, rugby players, and tennis players at Wimbledon switching from white shorts to dark colours), this prejudice is slowly diminishing. However, within orthodox Judaism, women continue to visit the *mikvah* – the ritual bath – at the end of each menstrual cycle – in order to (symbolically) purify themselves. But the mikvah isn't used exclusively for this purpose: men who are converting to Judaism are required to visit the bath, as are people recovering from serious illness; this helps to reduce the stigma that might otherwise be associated with menstruation.

However, in relation to time, menstruation remains a highly significant event. The very use of the word 'period' underlines the *temporal* nature of these regular changes in females' bodies from early teenage to the menopause (usually mid-40s to mid-50s) and refers to the part of the menstrual cycle when bleeding occurs (for most women every 28 days, although anywhere from 23–35 days is quite common). The menstrual cycle is the time from the first day of the woman's period to the day before her next period. This means that, for much of their adult life, women are always (unless pregnant) involved in a cyclical process of bodily processes; their 'time of the month' is a 'marker event' for which there's no male equivalent (but see below) and which, unlike most marker events, occurs both frequently and regularly.

Reproductive hormones (follicle-stimulating hormone, oestrogen, and progesterone) are the physiological basis of the menstrual cycle.[31] Both men and women, from puberty onwards, experience cyclical hormonal fluctuations; in fact, since hormone release is *pulsatile*, rather than continuous, there are marked minute-to-minute variations in hormone levels in both males and females.[32] Men's testosterone levels are cyclical in nature, although peaks and troughs aren't as predictable as oestrogen changes in women.[33]

Compared with research into women's hormonal cycles, there's relatively little study of the effects of testosterone in men. Several reasons for this difference have been identified, including[34]:

- The absence of cues associated with men's hormonal cycles;
- The tacit cultural belief that women's reproductive system exerts a powerful influence on female behaviour; this raises

questions concerning the value-free nature of scientific enquiry.[35]

Thus, while cyclicity is in fact the rule rather than the exception in living organisms, human female reproductive cyclicity, which is marked by menstruation, has attracted a disproportionate amount of modern research attention[36]

A much-cited study that claims to have demonstrated the *synchronization of female menstruation* is described in Box 5.2.

Box 5.2   Studies of menstrual synchrony[37]

- The synchronization of female menstruation was identified when it was observed that the menstrual cycle among 135 dormitory mates (aged 17–22) and friends (135 in total) became synchronized.
- Following further research, she concluded that this was caused by *pheromones* transmitted through social interaction. Pheromones are odourless chemical substances; when secreted by an individual into the environment, they produce specific reactions in others (usually of the same species). It was originally suggested there may be a specific female pheromone that affects the timing of others' menstrual cycles.[38]
- A ten-year longitudinal (follow-up) study of 29 women (aged 20–35) with a history of irregular, spontaneous ovulation was undertaken by the same research team.[39] Pheromone samples were taken from nine of the women at certain points in their menstrual cycles by placing cotton pads under their arms (worn for at least eight hours). The pads were then treated with alcohol (to disguise any smell) and frozen; they were then wiped under the noses of the 20 other women on a daily basis.

- Approximately 68 per cent of the women responded to the pheromones. Menstrual cycles were *reduced* (by 1–14 days) if the pheromones had been collected in the early stages of the donors' cycles (by speeding up their pre-ovulatory surge of luteinizing hormone). Pheromones collected later, during ovulation, *lengthened* the menstrual cycles by 1–12 days, by delaying the luteinizing hormone surge.
- The so-called 'McClintock effect' has been questioned, with some critics claiming that the findings could have occurred by chance alone.

GIVING BIRTH

'Birthing is an experience described and understood in time in Western societies. Questions like: 'How long between contractions?'; 'How long do your contractions last?'; 'What time did your waters break?'; 'How long was your labour?' shape both the medical and social discourses about labour and delivery. But contemporary accounts of birthing often focus on tensions in how time is understood and mediated in birth, with medical timelines understood to be generating birthing interventions, sometimes with adverse outcomes for women ...[40]

Natural birth advocates argue that women's bodies and needs must shape the temporal progression of birth, *not* medical timelines. Many accounts in Western countries distinguish between '*medical time*' and '*natural birthing time*'; this depicts a confict between (i) medical protocols for birthing (obstetrical control, with its focus on delineated birth stages and time limits, with the clock guiding expectations of progression through labour and delivery), and (ii) women's embodied experiences and physiological changes and birthing rhythms and expectations, respectively.

It has been suggested that obstetric measurement of observable birth signs and the use of time-based labour stages are at odds with the experience of women in labour who leave quantifiable time behind ('natural time').[41] In turn, this conflict reflects a broader conflict, between lived time and industrial time,[42], which has been exposed and explored by feminist scholars. For example, the process of industrialization has been critically linked to the development of new time consciousness in Western subjects: defined hours of employment and smaller timepieces facilitated the internalization of new time disciplines. This change was inherently gendered: as linear industrial time became the dominant temporal order (see above and Chapter 1), and was equated to the production of commodities, so women's reproductive labour becomes just one more such commodity (or, at least, the end product does). The process of birthing becomes highly routinized and time-regulated ('industrialized').[43]

Drawing on such contemporary feminist theoretical accounts of time, and based on interview data from a sample of Australian birthing women, the medical/natural time distinction has been acknowledged by a number of researchers. But this account of temporal conflict fails to capture the complexity96 of birthing time: a sense of temporal progress towards delivery is important to women in labour, as well as part of the medical model of birth. Women's experiences of birth cannot simply be understood in terms of conflicts between medical timelines and 'natural' birthing timings: women use communication about time to develop their own birth stories and generate a sense of progress and forward movement towards delivery.[44]

HOW DO MEN AND WOMEN SPEND THEIR TIME?

Given our discussion of 'Time is money' above and in Chapter 2, it's interesting to note that there have been recent efforts to measure poverty that try to expose poverty levels between individuals living under the same roof; this contrasts with the traditional approach that measures poverty at the household level. The focus of this new approach has been on *gender*.

The findings of a World Bank Report concerned with 'Gender and Development'[45] was updated some years later.[46] Both reports involved a broad sample of 19 countries and seven regions: Albania, Argentina, Bangladesh, Colombia, Ecuador, Ghana, Guatemala, Iraq, Mexico, Moldova, Mongolia, Pakistan, Peru, South Africa, Timor-Leste, Turkey, Uruguay, the US, and the West Bank and Gaza. They analyzed time use patterns across *market work* (paid and unpaid work for the production of goods and services sold in the market), unpaid childcare and domestic work, personal care activities, and leisure, social, and study activities over the lifecycle.

The findings confirmed popular perceptions: for men, getting married and having children means more time for leisure and earning money in the marketplace, while for women it means more unpaid childcare and domestic work, less leisure time, and less opportunity to earn in the marketplace.

These findings, compared with earlier studies, suggest that progress in reducing gender gaps in time use has been uneven. Some countries have made improvements in recent years, while differences persist – or have even widened – in others. Gender differences in time use can be a driving force of gender gaps in access to economic opportunities and, ultimately, a constraint on development. Evidence has shown that breaking out of this trap requires targeted policies to lift the constraints on women's time, increase their access to productive assets, and correct market and institutional failures.[47]

NOTES

1. Triandis (1990)
2. Moghaddam et al. (1993)
3. Gross (2019, p. 196)
4. Ezzell (2006)
5. Hofstede (1980)

6. Triandis op cit.; Triandis et al. (1986)
7. Rochat (2022, p. 216)
8. Fuentes (2017, p. 9)
9. Gross op cit (p. 193)
10. Owusu-Bempah & Howitt (2000)
11. Birth (1999)
12. Hall (1983)
13. Smith & Bond (1998)
14. Ibid.
15. Hofstede op cit.
16. Levine et al. (1980); Levine & Bartlett (1984)
17. Levine & Norenzayan (1999)
18. Levine & Bartlett (1984)
19. Lee & Duenas (1995)
20. Laungani (2007)
21. Zimbardo (2002) cited in Boniwell & Zimbardo (2003)
22. Ezzell op cit.
23. Cited in Ezzell, ibid.
24. Meade (1972)
25. Smith & Bond op cit.
26. Laungani op cit
27. Madan (1987)
28. Boroditsky (2011)
29. Boroditsky & Gaby (2010)
30. Miles et al. (2010)
31. Boroditsky op cit.
32. Muldoon & Reilly (1998)
33. Doering (1974)
34. Muldoon & Reilly op cit.
35. Tavris & Wade (1984)
36. Muldoon & Reilly op cit. (p. 59)
37. McClintock (1971, 1988)
38. McClintock (1971 op cit.)
39. McClintock & Stern (1988)
40. Maher (2008, p. 129)
41. Fox (1989) cited in Maher op cit.

42. Everingham (2002)

43. Davies (1990)

44. Maher *op cit.*

45. Rubiano-Matulvich, Carolina & Viollaz (2019)

46. Rubiano-Matulvich, Viollaz & Walsh (2019)

47. *Ibid.*

6

DEATH AND TIME
THE END OF TIME

We know that all living things eventually die, including animals and human beings. It's also widely believed that only human beings are aware of this fact of life and, according to many thinkers, this inevitably creates *death terror* as a feature of human existence (another fact of life). How we deal with death terror can take many forms, a major example being religious belief in an afterlife (or some equivalent view of immortality).

While death implies 'nothingness forever' (which is what makes death terror so powerful), immortality implies 'life forever' (which makes belief in an afterlife so appealing). However, before exploring these issues in more detail, it might be useful to consider a relatively neglected question, namely, what do we imagine it would be like to live forever?

For many people, this might seem like the best of all possible worlds; it would, of course, remove death terror as we currently experience it, because it would remove the inevitability of death from illness or old age (although it might still allow death resulting from natural disasters, violent crime etc.). However, wouldn't it at the same time undermine (the need for) belief in immortality as offered by belief in God?

Religious belief offers *literal* immortality (e.g. 'heaven'), while *symbolic* immortality has nothing to do with religion; it refers to all

DOI: 10.4324/9781032696218-6

those ways of being remembered after death (through producing offspring, leaving behind works of art or literature, or a myriad of other achievements or legacies). The crucial question is: without the certainty of death – and regardless of whether we experience death terror or how we deal with it – would we be motivated to work towards those achievements and legacies? Isn't the (implicit) knowledge of the finitude of life the underlying (albeit often unconscious) driving force for creative, scientific, interpersonal, and other accomplishments? Wouldn't life lose its purpose if we believed it was (potentially) infinite?

In the context of terror management theory (TMT):

> The awareness that we humans will die has a profound and pervasive effect on our thoughts, feelings, and behaviours in almost every domain of human life – whether we are conscious of it or not.

> Over the course of human history, the terror of death has guided the development of art, religion, language, economics, and science. It raised the pyramids in Egypt and razed the Twin Towers in Manhattan. It contributes to conflicts around the globe ...[1]

In an existential context, it has been suggested that the understanding of time is crucially important for humans: it provides a milieu/context in which goals and goal-related behaviour can exist. The knowledge that human life is finite (we are mortal beings who will cease to exist one day) represents a psychological burden that is uniquely carried by humans.[2] We may be better able to face the physical and psychological reality of mortality partly because we have a sense of past and future time periods (compared with non-human animals that live exclusively in the immediate present and so don't recognize past experiences or future possibilities.[3]

Without this 'mortality burden', would at least some people feel less driven to have children? While the motives for this are varied, and many people may not seriously question their motives but just see having offspring as 'natural', the 'legacy-value' of sons or daughters may be seriously undermined.

Of course, a world where death was not inevitable would be a very different place from what we currently know (or what previous generations knew); for example, overpopulation would be a far greater problem than it currently is, and the demands on the environment would be unimaginable. In other words, everything we know and understand about the world and how it 'works' – or, at least, our cultural version of it – and our predictions and expectations about it – rest on the inevitability of the death of every single individual, without exception. Death is a fact of life.

> Death exists because life exists, and vice versa. The reality of one defines the other ... most of what we do is in denial of death, therefore also in denial of what life is in essence: futile, fragile, and passing.

> Death is denied, first and foremost, by the instinctive and deeply ingrained drive to survive, reproduce, and keep life going. This is a necessary rule of nature, from plants, to bacteria, to gorillas. All living things do share the struggle to exist and reproduce. The denial of death is what keeps evolution and life going on this earth.[4]

CONSCIOUSNESS AND DEATH

Unique to humans is *higher-order consciousness*: the recognition by a thinking subject of his or her own actions or feelings, embodying a model of the personal, and of the past and future, as well as the present. We're conscious of being conscious.[5] This puts human beings in a 'privileged position'; this awareness of our own existence gives us a high degree of behavioural flexibility that helps us stay alive, reproduce, and pass our genes to future generations.[6]

However, there's a flip side to this privileged position. The existential psychotherapist Rollo May describes consciousness as both a blessing and a curse. Why a curse? Because we're the only species aware of the fact that we die, as well as having the capacity to question the purpose of what we do in and with our lives.[7] Similarly, Irvin Yalom, another famous existential psychotherapist states that:

> Self-awareness is a supreme gift, a treasure as precious as life. This is what makes us human. But it comes with a costly price: the wound of mortality. Our existence is forever shadowed by the knowledge that we will grow, blossom, and, inevitably, diminish and die.[8]

Yalom quotes from the 4,000-year-old Babylonian hero, Gilgamesh, reflecting on the death of his friend, Enkidu: 'Thou hast become dark and cannot hear me. When I die shall I not be like Enkidu? Sorrow enters my heart. I am afraid of death'.

> Gilgamesh speaks for all of us. As he feared death, so do we all – each and every man, woman, and child. For some of us the fear of death manifests only indirectly, either as generalized unrest or masqueraded as another psychological symptom; other individuals experience an explicit and conscious stream of anxiety about death; and for some of us the fear of death erupts into terror that negates all happiness and fulfillment.[9]

Our 'cherished gifts' (our unique capacity for language, culture, abstract thought, conscious self-reflection, thinking about the future and our long-term goals) come at a price:

> Our self-awareness and unparalleled foresight mean that we humans, unlike other animals, realise that we will all shuffle off this mortal coil sooner or later. This poses a potentially devastating challenge to our psychological equanimity – the

prospect of annihilation threatens to rob life of ultimate purpose, and render the pursuit of a meaningful life a futile effort.[10]

Having both an animal body and a symbolic self (self-consciousness) are two ways of being that are fundamentally incompatible – and uniquely human.[11]

It has been claimed that the uniquely human awareness of mortality is a by-product of self-consciousness, which otherwise provides remarkable adaptive advantages.[12] However, self-conscious creatures oriented towards survival in a threatening world but now burdened with awareness of their morality, might be overwhelmed by debilitating terror to the point of cognitive and behavioural paralysis – at which point self-consciousness would no longer confer an adaptive advantage. From now on, only those who developed and adopted *cultural world views* (CWVs) that could keep terror in check would enjoy evolutionary advantages provided by self-awareness. CWVs are humanly-constructed beliefs about reality shared by groups of individuals; they allow us to feel that we are significant contributors to a personal world, protecting us from the notion that we are merely purposeless animals that no longer exist following our death.

> Culture reduces anxiety by providing its constituents with a sense that they are valuable members of a meaningful universe. Meaning is derived from ... [CWVs] ... that offer an account of the origin of the universe, prescriptions of appropriate conduct, and guarantees of safety and security to those who adhere to such instructions – in this life and beyond, in the form of symbolic and/or literal immortality ...[13]

This account of the nature and function of CWVs is central to *terror management theory* (TMT).[14] Archaeological evidence, theory, and research from Evolutionary Psychology, anthropology, and cognitive neuroscience converge in supporting the claim that humans 'solved' the problems associated with realization of their mortality by creating uniquely human cultural products, including language, art, religion, agriculture, and economics.

SYMBOLIC AND LITERAL IMMORTALITY

Religious affiliations and identities provide a sense of symbolic continuance after bodily death (*symbolic immortality*) via enduring contributions to the religious community or its causes, or simply by identifying with the collective, which will endure beyond one's individual death. In this way, religions are very similar to secular (non-religious) forms of symbolic death transcendence, such as nations, the sciences, and the arts.[15] Contributions to these, as in great works of art or scientific achievement, can also produce symbolic immortality, as can amassing vast wealth or property – or 'simply' having children.[16]

What makes religions unique is that they also offer hope of *literal immortality*; they do this by: '... Providing people with supernatural conceptions of reality that include the possibility of transcending death through an immortal soul and afterlife ...'[17]

WHAT MAKES THE PROSPECT OF DEATH SO TERRIFYING?

While there is plenty of research evidence to support the basic assumptions and claims of TMT,[18] the core underlying assumption is that death terror is a real, inevitable, universal human phenomenon. Why should this be so?

In his powerful poem, *Aubade*, Philip Larkin refers to death as the 'extinction that we travel to and shall be lost in always'. The thought of being nowhere is a 'special way of being afraid' which religion's promise of immortality is no match for. But, the poem continues, surely, as rational beings, we cannot fear something we won't feel or see. However, this is precisely the point: the prospect of not sensing anything, not thinking anything, of complete and utter *nothingness* is what's so terrifying.[19]

Across generations, societies have approached and dealt with death in various ways, according to the era or environmental circumstances. In early human existence, nomadic group life perpetuated the likelihood of early death from disease, accident, lack of nutrition or predation.[20]

Although a highly common occurrence, the realization of personal death probably wasn't confronted consciously. But as *Homo sapiens* progressed as a species, evidence of the recognition of the *meaning* of death was displayed through deliberate burial with rites or possessions (beginning about 130,000 years ago). Perhaps the best-known example is the ancient Egyptians' use of mummification, which demonstrated the belief that they were ensuring that their loved ones' 'essence' passed to the afterlife.[21]

Greek and Buddhist philosophy ushered in an era of pondering the tensions between life and the inevitability of death. Indeed, it can be argued that all philosophy focuses on death; its primary focus on life and the components of life that are worthwhile is inherently located within the context of death: 'death is truly the inspiring genius of philosophy'.[22]

According to Epicurus, one of the ancient Greek philosophers, the root cause of human misery is our omnipresent fear of death: '... the frightening vision of inevitable death interferes with one's enjoyment of life and leaves no pleasure undisturbed ...'[23] Epicurus also dismissed the fear of *non-being* in death as *irrational*:

i. the soul is mortal and so, when consciousness no longer exists, so will the ability to recognize one's past, present, and future;

ii. following the death of the body and soul, perception ceases and we cannot fear what we cannot perceive;

iii. we inevitably return to the state in which we existed before conception/birth, a state of 'non-existence'/'non-beingness'; as we have no recollection of this, there's nothing to fear.

Regarding (iii), this is the argument that Larkin addresses and powerfully rejects in *Aubade*: death terror stems from – and *can* only stem from – the consciousness we have *now*:

> ... in between the time before we existed and after we no longer exist, we are conscious, thinking beings, with the ability to contemplate a future in which the awareness of and participation in the world will one day cease. We're comparing this future non-being with our *present* consciousness (which includes thinking about our future non-existence), *not* with those aeons of time before we existed. It is mistaken to equate the before and after states ...[24]

With regard to the 'before', there's nothing *to* contemplate, and it's almost impossibly difficult – although theoretically possible – to contemplate the 'after': we can only contemplate non-existence if *we exist and are conscious*. The harder we try to imagine non-existence, the harder it becomes: it requires the negation of the very act of imagination!

> ... Added to this is the affective response to the prospect of non-existence; it goes against the biological/evolutionary grain, the very powerful urge to live/survive.[25]

It's a widely-held belief that death terror is natural and universal, the fundamental fear that influences all others; however well we disguise it, no one is immune.[26] William James called death 'the worm at the core' of man's pretensions to happiness.[27] It has been claimed that most people think fear of death is absent because it rarely shows its true face: underneath all appearances, fear of death is universally present:

> For behind the sense of insecurity in the face of danger, behind the sense of discouragement and depression, there always lurks the basic fear of death, a fear which undergoes

most complex elaborations and manifests itself in many different ways ... No one is free of the fear of death ... The anxiety neuroses, the various phobic states, even a considerable number of depressive suicidal states and many schizophrenias amply demonstrate the ever-present fear of death which become woven into the major conflicts of the given psychopathological conditions ... We may take for granted that the fear of death is always present in our mental functioning.[28]

Adopting a Darwinian (evolutionary) perspective, this fear can be understood as an expression of the instinct of *self-preservation*; this functions as a constant drive to maintain life and to master the dangers that threaten life:

Such constant expenditure of psychological energy on the business of preserving life would be impossible if the fear of death were not as constant. The very term 'self-preservation' implies an effort against some force of disintegration: the affective aspect of this is fear, fear of death.[29]

In other words, the fear of death must be present behind all our normal functioning, in order for us to be equipped for self-preservation. But this fear cannot be present constantly in our conscious mental functioning, otherwise we simply couldn't function.[30]

... It must be properly *repressed* to keep us living with any modicum of comfort. We know very well that to repress means more than to put away and to forget that which was put away and ... where we put it. It means also to maintain a constant psychological effort to keep the lid on and inwardly never relax our watchfulness.[31]

GRIEF AND TIME

Another way of trying to answer the question as to why the prospect – and inevitability – of death is so terrifying is to look at it in the context of separation and grief.

John Bowlby, the influential British psychoanalyst, regarded adult grief as a form of *separation anxiety*, first observed in young children when separated from an attachment figure (in particular, the mother-figure).[32]

> Psychologically, death is separation ... the absolute and irreversible silence of others to whom we depend and are attached to. It is a looming fact and an eventuality that we dread, a rational inference and anticipation, especially if you don't have particular transcendental beliefs in an afterlife ...[33]

This fear of 'losing' loved ones through their death is one side of a coin; the flip side is our own death, in which we leave behind '... all of what we grew attached to, all the things and people we developed to depend on: our life made of friends, family, projects, comfort, excitement, perceptions, feelings, or ideas ...[34]

So, part of death terror is the anticipated loss of all those 'things '– relationships, feelings, memories, beliefs, etc. – that make us 'us'. However much we hope and believe that others will remember us after our death, there's only so much – and only certain kinds of things – that they ever could remember. Perhaps the relatively recent popularity of writing memoirs can be understood as people's attempts to leave behind parts of themselves that only they could; this way, the more subjective, private parts of the self become memorable (in a literal sense), a form of symbolic immortality that has been produced for that very purpose (consciously or unconsciously).

While (the prospect of) the death of a loved one is painful and requires a huge adjustment on the part of the bereaved, some bereavements are more painful – and more difficult to come to terms with – than others. If people were asked to create a hierarchy of pain in relation to different relationships, it would be highly likely that, at least in the case of parents, loss of their child(ren) would come out on top.

Chronologically, and statistically, we expect to die before our children (or nieces/nephews): it runs against the 'natural order' to outlive our children (regardless of cause of death). '... To most people in the west, the death of a child is the most agonizing and distressing source of grief':[35] it's untimely and non-normative, and is often traumatic, sudden, and sometimes inexplicable (as in sudden infant death syndrome/SIDS). In Developing countries, women continue to have large families, because they expect many of their children to die; here, the death of a child – especially in infancy – is less psychologically devastating than it is in Western countries.[36]

Another popular publishing trend in recent years is personal accounts by bereaved individuals of their 'grief journey'; some of these have been written by well-known authors (including C.S. Lewis, Danne Abse, and Julian Barnes) but increasingly these accounts are written by first-time authors, driven to describe their grief in print both as a way of dealing with their pain and as a form of dedication to their loved one. Two quite recent examples deserve a mention, and are especially relevant to the theme of this book.

5,742 Days is the title of Anne-Marie Cockburn's (2013) account of her 15-year-old daughter's life: she lived for 5,742 days.[37] Denise Riley, an eminent poet and philosopher, records her response to the death of her adult son in Time Lived Without Its Flow (2019); this is written as a diary, a 'real-time' account of her evolving grief.[38]

The central 'thesis' of Riley's book concerns the strange way in which sequential time is stopped following a sudden death (her son was found dead in a still-running bath, having possibly had a heart attack); in one sense, there's no 'after' and she finds herself 'trapped' in the present. It is as if she has died, and yet she is more alive than ever: at two weeks post-bereavement, she writes:

You share in the death of your child, in that you approach it so closely that you sense that a part of you, too, has died that instant. At the same time, you feel that the spirit of the child has leaped into you. So you are both partly dead and yet more alive. You are cut down, and yet you burn with life.[39]

The six months entry begins like this:

A summer has gone, a cold autumn is setting in, but I've no sense of my time as having any duration, or any future. Time now is a plateau. I only know whether an event came before or after the date of the death ...[40]

After her final ('three years after') entry, Riley tries to expand on what 'time lived without flow' really means. She talks about the 'dislocation in the experienced time' of those left behind following the sudden death of a child; they are thrown into 'timeless time' or 'non-time',[41] a state of 'a-chronicity'. But, perhaps surprisingly, this can be to enter a '... not unpleasant state of tremendous simplicity, of easy candour and bright emptiness'.[42] This isn't a reflective state of mind, but a bodily sensation as real and inescapable as feeling thirsty.

The irony is that this strong experience resurrects the life in the dead metaphor of 'time stopped' – while the occasion for this linguistic reanimation, the formerly living child – stays stubbornly dead.[43]

As extreme a life-changing event as bereavement can be, it is perhaps one of many that we use to chart our course through life: when trying to locate some event in time, we may initially narrow down the time frame by asking if it was likely to have taken place 'before or after X', 'X' standing for any marker event (such as starting/leaving school or university, being in a particular job, meeting our future partner, having a particular illness or publishing our first book). In parallel, we carve up our lives into 'before'/'after' chunks, based on our view of time as linear: the biggest 'chunks' are something like the developmental stages we identified in Chapter 1; each of these is then broken down into smaller 'before'/'after' chunks until we zoom in on the event we're trying to locate.

Our ability to *mentally time travel* allows us to view what was once 'present' or 'future' as 'past: our past consists of a large number of interrelated 'pasts', 'presents', and 'futures' but we must wait for the future to know how the past has unfolded.

NOTES

1. Solomon, Greenberg & Pyszczynski (2015)
2. Becker (1962)
3. Vohs & Baumeister (2004)
4. Rochat (2022)
5. Edelman (1992)
6. Solomon, Greenberg & Pyszczynski *op cit.*
7. Yalom (2008)
8. *Ibid.* (pp. 1–2)
9. Jones (2008)
10. *Ibid.* (p. 581)
11. Becker *op cit.*
12. Becker (1973)
13. Solomon, Greenberg, & Pyszczynski (2004)
14. *Ibid*; Solomon, Greenberg & Pyszczynski (2015) *op cit.*
15. Greenberg et al. (2020)
16. Solomon, Greenberg, & Pyszczynski (2004) *op cit.*
17. Greenberg et al. *op cit.*
18. *Ibid*; Solomon, Greenberg, & Pyszczynski (2004/2015) *op cit.*
19. Larkin (1977)
20. Spellman (2014)
21. *Ibid.*
22. Kubler-Ross (1975, p.2)
23. Yalom *op cit.*

24. Gross (2023, p. 187)
25. Ibid. (p. 187)
26. Becker (1973) *op cit.*
27. James (1902, p. 121)
28. Zilboorg (1943, pp. 466–7)
29. Ibid. (p. 467)
30. Becker (1973) *op cit.*
31. Zilboorg *op cit.* (p. 467)
32. Bowlby (1980)
33. Rochat *op cit.* (p. 248)
34. Ibid. (p. 248)
35. Parkes (2006)
36. Scheper-Hughes (1992)
37. Cockburn (2013)
38. Riley (2019)
39. Ibid. (p. 20)
40. Ibid. (p. 26)
41. Ibid. (p. 56)
42. Ibid. (p. 57)
43. Ibid. (p. 58)

REFERENCES

Andreasen, N.C. & Pierson, R. (2008) The role of the cerebellum in schizophrenia. *Biological Psychiatry*, 64(2), 81–8.

Banks, W.P. & Pockett, S. (2007) Benjamin Libet's work on the neuroscience of
free will. In M. Velmans & S. Schneider (eds.) *The Blackwell Companion to
Consciousness*. Oxford: Blackwell Publishing.

Becker, E. (1962) *The Birth and Death of Meaning*. New York: Free Press.

Becker, E. (1973) *The Denial of Death*. New York: Free Press.

Bentall, R.P. (2007) Researching psychotic complaints. *The Psychologist*, 20(5),
293–5.

Bergson, H. (1889) *Time and Free Will: An Essay on the Immediate Data of Consciousness*.
London: George Allen & Unwin (trans. F.L. Podgson).

Binofski, F. & Block, R. (1996) Accelerated time experience after left frontal
cortex lesion. *Neurocase*, 2, 485–93.

Birth, K.K. (1999) *Any Time Is Trinidad Time: Social Meanings and Temporal Consciousness*.
University of Florida Press.

Blakemore, C. (1988) *The Time Machine*. London: BBC Books.

Blakemore, S.J., Smith, J., Steel, R. et al. (2000) The perception of self-
produced sensory stimuli in patients with auditory hallucinations and
passivity experiences. *Psychological Medicine*, 30, 1131–39.

Boniwell, L. & Zimbardo, P. (2003) Time to find the right balance. *The
Psychologist*, 16(3), 129–31.

Boroditsky, L. (2000) Metaphoric structuring: Understanding time through spatial metaphors. *Cognition*, 75, 1–28.

Boroditsky, L. (2011) How language shapes thought. *Scientific American*, 304(2), 42–5.

Boroditsky, L. & Gaby, A. (2010) Remembrance of times east: Absolute spatial representations of time in an Australian aboriginal community. *Psychological Science*, 21(11), 1635–9.

Boroditsky, L. & Ramscar, M. (2002) The roles of body and mind in abstract thought. *Psychological Science*, 13, 185–8.

Bowlby, J. (1980) *Attachment and Loss: Loss.* Harmondsworth: Penguin.

Bradburn, N.M., Rips, L.J. & Shevell, S. (1987) Answering autobiographical questions: the impact of memory and inference on surveys. *Science*, 236(4798), 157–61.

Brown, A.S. (2004) Getting to grips with déjà vu. *The Psychologist*, 17(12), 694–6.

Brown, G. (2007) The bitter end. *New Scientist*, 196(2625), 42–3.

Brown, R. & Kulik, J. (1977) Flashbulb memories. *Cognition*, 5, 73–99.

Busch, N.A., Dubois, J. & Van Rullen, R. (2009) The phase of ongoing EEG oscillations predicts visual perception. *Journal of Neuroscience*, 29, 7869.

Callender, C. (2010) Is time an illusion? *Scientific American*, 302(6), 40–7.

Callender, C. (2012) Is time an illusion? *Scientific American Special Edition*, 21(1), 14–21.

Camus, A. (1942/2005) *The Myth of Sisyphus.* London: Penguin. (Originally published in French, 1942; first English translation, 1955).

Carter, R. (2006) The limits of imagination. In R. Headlam Wells & J. McFadden (eds.) *Human Nature: Fact and Fiction.* London: Continuum.

Cavanagh, K. (2000) Internal clocks and human timing. *The Psychologist*, 13(2), 82–3.

Chomsky, N. (1965) *Aspects of the Theory of Syntax.* Cambridge, MA: MIT Press.

Cockburn, A-M. (2013) *5, 742 Days: A Mother's Journey Through Loss.* Oxford: Infinite Ideas Limited.

Cohen, N.J. & Squire, L.R. (1980) Preserved learning and retention of pattern-analysing skills in amnesia: Dissociation of knowing how from knowing that. *Science*, 210, 207–10.

Colman, A.M. (2008) *Oxford Dictionary of Psychology.* Oxford: Oxford University Press.

Coniam, M. (2001) Rodents to freedom. Philosophy Now, 32, 10–11.

Conway, M.A. (1990) Autobiographical Memory. Milton Keynes: Open University Press.

Corballis, M. (2011) The Recursive Mind: The Origins of Human Language, Thought, and Civilization. Princeton, NJ: Princeton University Press.

Corballis, M. & Suddendorf, T. (2007) Memory, Time, Language. In C. Pasternak (ed.) What Makes Us Human? Oxford: Oneworld.

Crawley, S.E. & Pring, L. (2000) When did Mrs Thatcher resign? The effects of ageing on the dating of public events. Memory, 8, 111–21.

Damasio, A.R. (2006) Remembering when. Scientific American Special Edition: A Matter of Time, 16(1), 34–41.

Damasio, A.R. (2012) Remembering When. Scientific American: A Matter of Time, 21(1), 42–7.

Davies, K. (1990) Women, Time and the Weaving of the Strands of Everyday Life. Avebury.

Deacon, T.W. (1997) The symbolic species: The co-evolution of language and the brain. New York: W.W. Norton.

Doering, C.H. (1974) Plasma testosterone levels and psychological measures in men over a two-year period. In R.C. Friedman, R.M. Richart & R.L. Varde Wiele (eds.) Sex Differences in Behaviour. New York: Wiley.

Dong, X., Milholland, B. & Vijg, J. (2016) Evidence for a limit to human lifespan. Nature, 538, 257–259.

Draaisma, D. (2004) Why Life Speeds Up As You Get Older: How Memory Shapes Our Past. Cambridge: Cambridge University Press.

Eagleman, D.M. & Pariyadat, V. (2009) Is subjective duration a signature of coding efficiency? Philosophical Transactions of the Royal Society B, 364, 1841–51.

Eagleman, D.M. & Pariyadat, V. (2010) Duration illusions and what they tell us about the brain. In N. Srinivasan, B.R. Kar & J. Pandey (eds.) Advances in Cognitive Science, Vol.2. Delhi: Sage Publications.

Edelman, G. (1989) The Remembered Present: A Biological Theory of Consciousness. New York: Basic Books.

Edelman, G. (1992) Bright Air, Brilliant Fire: On the Matter of the Mind. Harmondsworth: Penguin.

Einstein, A. (1905) Zur Elektrodynamik bewegter Korper. Annalen der Physik, 17, 891–921.

Einstein, A. (1916) Die Grundlage der algemeinen Relativitats theorie. *Annalen der Physik*, 49, 769–822.

Eiser, J.R. (1994) *Attitudes, Chaos and the Connectionist Mind*. Oxford: Blackwell.

Empson, J. (1993) *Sleep and Dreaming* (2nd revised edition). Hemel Hempstead: Harvester Wheatsheaf.

Enoch, D. & Ball, H. (2001) *Uncommon Psychiatric Syndromes* (4th edition). London: Arnold.

Everingham, C. (2002) Engendering Time Gender equity and discourses of workplace flexibility. *Time & Society*, 11(2–3), 335–51.

Ezzell, C. (2006) Clocking Cultures. *Scientific American Special Edition: A Matter of Time*, 16(1), 42–5.

Fancher, R.E. & Rutherford, A. (2012) *Pioneers of Psychology* (4th edition). New York: W.W. Norton & Co., Inc.

Fitzgerald, J.M. (1992) Autobiographical memory and conceptualizations of the self. In M.A. Conway, D.C. Rubin, H. Spinnler, & W.A. Wagenaar (eds.) *Theoretical Perspectives in Autobiographical Memory*. Dordrecht: Kluwer Academic Publishers.

Ford, J.M. & Mathalon, D.H. (2004) Electrophysiological evidence of corollary discharge dysfunction in schizophrenia during talking and thinking. *Journal of Psychiatric Research*, 38, 37–46.

Fox, D. (2009) The time machine in your head. *New Scientist*, 204(2731), 32–37.

Fraisse, P. (1964) *The Psychology of Time*. London: Eyre & Spottiswoode.

Frankenheuser, M. (1959) *Estimation of Time: An Experimental Study*. Stockholm: Almqvist & Wiksell.

French, C. C. (2005) Near-death experiences in cardiac arrest survivors. *Progress in Brain Research*, 150, 351–367. 10.1016/S0079-6123(05)50025-6.

Freud, S. (1900/1976a) *The Interpretation of Dreams*. Pelican Freud Library (4) Harmondsworth: Penguin.

Fromholt, P. & Larsen, S.E. (1992) Autobiographical memory and life-history narratives in ageing and dementia (Alzheimer type). In M.A. Conway, D.C. Rubin, H. Spinnler & W.A. Wagenaar (eds.) *Perspectives in Autobiographical Memory*. Dordrecht: Kluwer Academic Publishers.

Fromm, E. (1941) *Escape from Freedom*. Oxford: Farrar & Rinehart.

Fuentes, A. (2017) *The Creative Spark: How Imagination Made Humans Exceptional*. New York: Dutton.

Gallagher, S. (2007) Phenomenological approaches to consciousness. In M. Velmans & S. Schneider (eds.) *The Blackwell Companion to Consciousness*. Oxford: Blackwell Publishing.

Galton, F. (1879) Psychometric experiments. *Brain*, 2, 149–62.

Gamble, J. (2013) Into Darkness. *New Scientist*, 220(2945), 38–9.

Gerstner, G.E. & Fazio, V.A. (1995) Evidence for a universal perceptual unit in mammals. *Ethology*, 101, 89–100.

Gould, R.L. (1978) *Transformations: Growth and Change in Adult Life*. New York: Simon & Schuster.

Gould, R.L. (1980) Transformational tasks in adulthood. In S.I. Greenspan & G.H. Pollock (eds.) *The Course of Life: Psychoanalytic Contributions Toward Understanding Personality Development, Volume 3*: Adulthood and the Ageing Process. Washington, DC: National Institute for Mental Health.

Greenberg, J., Helm, P.J., Landau, M.J. & Solomon, S. (2020) Dwelling forever in the house of the lord: on the terror management function of religion. In K.E. Vail & C. Routledge (eds.) *The Science of Religion, Spirituality, and Existentialism*. London: Academic Press.

Gross, R. (2019) *Being Human: Psychological Perspectives on Human Nature* (2nd edition). London: Routledge.

Gross, R. (2020) *Psychology: The Science of Mind and Behaviour* (8th edition). London: Hodder Education.

Gross, R. (2023) *Themes, Issues and Debates in Psychology* (5th edition). London: Routledge.

Hall, E.T. (1983) *The Dance of Life*. New York: Doubleday.

Hammond, C. (2012) *Time Warped: Unlocking the Mysteries of Time Perception*. Edinburgh: Canongate.

Hartcollis, P. (1983) *Time and Timelessness: or, the Varieties of Temporal Experience*. New York: International Universities Press.

Heidegger, M. (1927/2008) *Being and Time*. London: SCM Press.

Heidegger, M. (1935/1983) Einfuhrung in die Metaphysik. In *Gesamtausgabe*. Vol. XL. Frankfurt am Main: Klostermann.

Herskovits, M.J. (1955) *Cultural Anthropology*. New York: Knopf.

Hirschfeld, L.A. & Gelman, S.D.A. (1994) *Mapping the Mind: Domain Specificity in Cognitive Development*. Cambridge, MA: Cambridge University Press.

Hofstede, G. (1980) *Culture's Consequences: International differences in work-related values*. London: Sage.

Husserl, E. (1928; trans.1991) *On the Phenomenology of the Consciousness of Internal Time* (1893-1917). The Hague: Kluwer.

Jackson, J. H. (1888) On a particular variety of epilepsy "intellectual aura", one case with symptoms of organic brain disease. *Brain*, 11, 179–207.

James, W. (1890) *The Principles of Psychology*. London: MacMillan.

James, W., (1902) *The Varieties of Religious Experience*. New York: Longman, Green & Co.

Jansari, A. & Parkin, A.J. (1996) Things that go bump in your life: Explaining the reminiscence bump in autobiographical memory. *Psychology and Ageing*, 11, 85–91.

Jones, D. (2008) Running to catch the sun. *The Psychologist*, 21(7), 580–3.

Jones, L.A. (2019) The Perception of Duration and the Judgement of the Passage of Time (pp. 53–67). In V. Arstila, A. Bardon, S.E. Power & A. Vatakis (eds.) *The Illusions of Time: Philosophical and psychological Essays on Timing and Time Perception*. Palgrave Macmillan.

Kant, I. (1781/1998) *Critique of Pure Reason*. New York: Cambridge University Press.

Kant, I. (1783/1950) *Prolegomena to any future metaphysics*. Indianapolis: Bobbs-Merrill.

Kant, I. (1787/1996) *Critique of Pure Reason*. trans. Pluhar, W.S. Indianapolis: Hackett Publishing Co.

Kemmerer, D. (2005) The spatial and temporal meanings of English prepositions can be independently impaired. *Neuropsychologica*, 43, 797–806.

Kierkegaard, S. (1844) *The Concept of Dread*. (Trans. W. Lowrie 1944). Princeton, NJ: Princeton University Press.

King, R.A. (2021) The Irrelevance of Time in Near-Death Experiences. *Academia Letters*, Article 2427. 10.20935/AL2427.

Kleitman, N. (1939) *Sleep and Wakefulness: As Alternating Phases in the Cycle of Existence*. Chicago, IL: University of Chicago Press.

Koch, C. (2020) What near-death experiences reveal about the brain. *Scientific American*. https://www.scientificamerican.com/article/what-near-death-experiences-reveal-about-ther-brain/

Korner, S. (1955) *Kant*. London: Penguin Books.

Kubler-Ross, E. (1975) *Death: The Final Stage of Growth*. New York: Simon & Schuster.

Lakoff, G. & Johnson, M. (1980) *Metaphors We Live By*. Chicago, IL: University of Chicago Press.

Larkin, P. (1977) Aubade. *Times Literary Supplement*, 23 December.

Laungani, P.D. (2007) *Understanding Cross-Cultural Psychology*. London: Sage.

Lee, Y.T. & Duenas, G. (1995) Stereotype accuracy in multicultural business. In Y.T. Lee, L.J. Jussim & C.R. McCauley (eds.) *Stereotype Accuracy: Towards appreciaiting group differences*. Washington: American Psychological Association.

Levine, R.V. & Bartlett, C. (1984) Pace of life, punctuality and coronary heart disease in six countries. *Journal of Cross-Cultural Psychology*, 15, 233–55.

Levine, R.V. & Norenzayan, A. (1999) The Pace of Life in 31 countries. *Journal of Crtoss-Cultural Psychology*, 30(2), 178–205.

Levine, R.V., West, L.J. & Reis, H.T. (1980) Perceptions of time and punctuality in the US and Brazil. *Journal of Personality & Social Psychology*, 38, 541–50.

Levinson, D.J., Darrow, D.N., Klein, E.B. et al. (1978) *The Seasons of a Man's Life*. New York: A.A. Knopf.

Libet, B. (1985) Unconscious cerebral initiative and the role of conscious will in voluntary action. *Behavioural & Brain Sciences*, 8, 529–66.

Libet, B. (1994) A testable field theory of mind-brain interaction. *Journal of Consciousness Studies*, 1, 119–26.

Libet, B. (2004) *Mind Time: The Temporal Factor in Consciousness*. Cambridge, MA: Harvard University Press.

Libet, B., Gleason, C.A., Wright, E.W. & Pearl, D.K. (1983) Time of conscious intention to act in relation to onset of cerebral activity (readiness potential): The unconscious initiation of a freely voluntary act. *Brain*, 106, 623–42.

Loehlin, J.C. (1959) The influence of different activities on the apparent length of time. *Psychological Monograph*, 73, 4.

Madan, T.N. (1987) *Non-renunciation: Themes and interpretations of Hindu culture*. Delhi: Oxford University Press.

Maher, J. (2008) Progressing through labour and delivery: Birth time and women's experiences. *Women's Studies International Forum*, 31(2), 129–37.

Mangan, p.a. (1996) *Report for the Annual Meeting of the Society for Neuroscience*. Washington, DC: Society for Neuroscience.

Manhart, K. (2004) The limits of multitasking. *Scientific American Mind*, 14(5), 62–7.

Matell, M.S. & Meck, W.H. (2000) Neuropsychological mechanisms of Interval Timing. *BioEssays*, 22(1), 94–103.

May, R. (1969) *Love and Will*. New York: Norton.

McClintock, M. (1971) Menstrual synchrony and suppression. *Nature*, 291, 244–5.

McClintock, M. (1988) On the nature of mammalian and human pheromones, olfaction and taste. *XII Annals of the New York Academy of Sciences*, 855, 390–2.

McClintock, M. & Stern, K. (1988) Regulation of Ovulation by Human Pheromones. *Nature*, 12, 177–9.

McCormack, P.D. (1979) Autobiographical memory in the aged. *Canadian Journal of Psychology*, 33, 118–24.

McKellar, P. (1968) *Experience and Behaviour*. Harmondsworth: Penguin.

McKellar, P. (1957) *Imagination and Thinking*. London: Cohen & West.

Meade, R.D. (1972) Future time perspectives of Americans and subcultures in India. *Journal of Cross-Cultural Psychology*, 3, 93–100.

Merleau-Ponty, M. (1964) *The primacy of perception*. Evanston, IL: Northwestern University Press.

Miller, A.D. & Goodale, M. (1997) *The Visual Brain in Action* (2nd edition). New York: Oxford University Press.

Miles, L., Nind, L.& Macrae, N. (2010) Moving through time. *Psychological Science*, published online 8 January.

Milner, A.D. & Goodale, M.A. (1995) *The Visual Brain in Action*. Oxford: Oxford University Press.

Moghaddam, F.M., Taylor, D.M. & Wright, S.C. (1993) *Social Psychology in Cross-Cultural Perspective*. New York: W.H. Freeman.

Moody, F.R. (1975) *Life after Life*. Covinda, GA: Mockingbird.

Muldoon, O. & Reilly, J. (1998) Biology. In K. Trew & J. Kremer (eds.) *Gender & Psychology*. London: Arnold.

Neppe, V.M. (1983) *The Psychology of Déjà vu: Have I Been Here Before?* Johannesburg: Witwatersrand University Press.

Newton, I. (1687) *Principia (Mathematical Principles of Natural Philosophy)*. Cambridge: Cambridge University Library Newton Manuscripts, Series 2.

Ogden, R.S. (2020) The passage of time during the UK Covid-19 lockdown. 10.1371/journal.pone.0235871.

Ogden, R.S. & Jones, L.A. (2009) More is still better: Testing the perturbation model of temporal reference memory across different modalities and tasks. *Quarterly Journal of Experimental Psychology*, 62(5), 909–924.

Orwell, G. (1949) *Nineteen Eighty Four*. Harmondsworth: Penguin.

Owusu-Bempah, K. & Howitt, D. (2000) *Psychology beyond Western Perspectives*. Leicester: British Psychological Society.

Parkes, C.M. (2006) *Love and Loss: The Roots of Grief and its Complications*. London: Routledge.

Pinker, S. (1994) *The Language Instinct*. New York: Morrow.

Pinker, S. (1997) *How the Mind Works*. London: Penguin Books.

Pinker, S. (2007) *The Stuff of Thought*. London: Penguin Books.

Pöppel, E. (1997) A hierarchical model of temporal perception. *Trends in Cognitive Sciences*, 1, 56–61.

Pöppel, E. (2004) Lost in time: A horizontal frame, elementary processing units and the 3-second window. *Acta Neurobiologiae Experimentalis*, 64, 295–301.

Pöppel, E. (2009) Pre-semantically defined temporal windows for cognitive processing. *Philosophical Transactions of the Royal Society B*, 364(1525), 1887–96.

Pöppel, E. & Logothetis, N. (1986) Neural oscillations in the human brain: Discontinuous initiations of pursuit eye movements indicate a 30-Hz temporal framework for visual information processing. *Naturwissenschaften* 73, 267–8.

Power, S.E. (2021) *Philosophy of Time: A Contemporary Introduction*. New York: Routledge.

Riley, D. (2019) *Time Lived, Without Its Flow*. London: Picador.

Rochat, P. (2022) *Finitude: The Psychology of Self and Time*. New York: Routledge.

Rovelli, C. (2018) *The Order of Time*. London: Penguin Random House.

Rubiano-Matulevich, E., Carolina, E. & Viollaz, M. (2019) *Gender Differences in Time Use. Allocating Time between the Market and the Household*. Research Working Paper (WPS 8981). Washington, DC: World Bank Group.

Rubiano-Matulevich, E., Viollaz, M. & Walsh, C. (2019) *Time after time: How men and women spend their time ands what it means for individual and household poverty and wellbeing*. Published on Data Blog (/opendata).

Rubin, D.C. & Schulkind, M.D. (1997) The distribution of autobiographical memories across the lifespan. *Memory and Cognition*, 25, 859–66.

Saavedra, V. (1968) *Rev. Neuropsichait.*, 31, 145.

Sartre, J.-P. (1943/1956) *Being and Nothingness*. Secaucus, NJ: Citadel Press.

Scheper-Hughes, N. (1992) *Death Without Weeping: The Violence of Everyday Life in Brazil*. Berkeley, CA: University of California Press.

Sheehy, G. (1976) *Passages: Predictable Crises of Adult Life*. New York: Bantam Books.

Shum, M.S. (1998) The role of temporal landmarks in autobiographical memory processes. *Psychological Bulletin*, 124, 423–42.

Siffre, M. (1975) Six months alone in a cave. *National Geographic*, March, 426–35.

Skowranski, J.J. & Thompson, C.P. (1990) Reconstructing dates of personal events: Gender differences in accuracy. *Applied Cognitive Psychology*, 4, 371–81.

Smith, P.B. & Bond, M.H. (1998) *Social Psychology Across Cultures* (2nd edition). Hemel Hempstaead: Harvester Wheatsheaf.

Solomon, S., Greenberg, J. & Pyszczynski, T. (2004) The cultural animal: Twenty years of terror management theory and research. In J. Greenberg, S.L. Koole & T. Pyszczynski (eds.) *Handbook of Experimental Existential Psychology*. New York: Guilford Press.

Solomon, S., Greenberg, J. & Pyszczynski, T. (2015) *The Worm at the Core: On the role of death in life*. London: Penguin Random House.

Spatt, J. (2002) Déjà vu: Possible parahippocampal mechanisms. *Journal of Neuropsychiatry and Clinical Neuroscience*, 14, 6–10.

Spellman, W.M. (2014) *A Brief History of Death*. London: Reaktion Books.

Spinney, L. (2018) Adventurer in Time. *New Scientist*, 230(3190), 40–1.

Stetson, C., Fiesta, M.P. & Eagleman, D. (2007) Does time really slow down during a frightening event? *PLoS ONE*, 2(12), pe:1295 (doi:10.1371/journal.pone.0001295).

Stevenson, A. (2020) *Cultural Issues in Psychology: An Introduction to a Global Discipline* (2nd edition). London: Routledge.

Suddendorf, T. & Corballis, M.C. (2007) The evolution of foresight|: What is mental time travel and is it unique to humans? *Behavioural and Brain Sciences*, 30, 299–313.

Suddendorf, T., Redshaw, J. & Bulley, A. (2022) *The Invention of Tomorrow: A Natural History of Foresight*. New York: Basic Books.

Sully, J. (1881) *Illusion: A Psychological Study*. London: Kegan Paul.

Tavris, C. & Wade, C. (1984) *The Longest War: Sex Differences in Perspective*. San Diego, CA: Harcourt, Brace, Jovanovich.

Taylor, S. (2020) When Seconds Turn into Minutes: Time Expansion Experiences in Altered States of Consciousness. *Journal of Humanistic Psychology*, 62(2), 208–32. 10.1177/0022167820917484.

Taylor, S. (2021) In a different timeworld. *The Psychologist*, 32–36, April.

Triandis, H.C. (1990) Theoretical concepts that are applicable to the analysis of ethnocentrism. In R.W. Brislin (ed.) *Applied Cross-Cultural Psychology*. Newbury Park, CA: Sage.

Triandis, H.C., Bontempo, R., Betancourt, H. et al. (1986) The measurement of etic aspects of individualism and collectivism across cultures. *Australian Journal of Psychology*, 38, 257–67.

Triandis, H.C., Bontempo, R., Villareal, M.J. et al. (1988) Individualism and collectivism: Cross-cultural perspectives on self-group relationships. *Journal of Personality & Social Psychology*, 54, 323–338.

Tulving, E. (1972) Episodic and semantic memory. In E. Tulving & W. Donaldson (eds.) *Organisation of Memory*, New York: Academic Press.

Tulving, E. (1985) Memory and consciousness. *Canadian Psychology*, 26, 1–12.

Van Rullen, R., Pascual-Leone, A. & Battelli, L. (2008) The Continuous Wagon Wheel Illusion and the 'When' Pathway of the right parietal lobe: A repetitive transcranial magnetic stimulation study. *PLoS ONE*, 3(8) pe2911 (doi:10.137/journal.pone.0002911).

Vierordt, von K. (1868) *Der Zeitsinn nach Versuchen*. Tubingen, Germany: Laupp. (Cited in Lejeune, H. & Wearden, J. (2009) Vierordt's The Experimental Study of the Time Sense (1868) and its legacy. *European Journal of Cognitive Psychology*, 21(6), 941–960.

Vohs, K.D. & Baumeister, R.F. (2004) Understanding self-regulation: An Introduction. In R.F.Baumeister & K.D.Vohs (eds.) *Handbook of Self-Regulation: Research, Theory and Applications*. New York: The Guilford Press.

Walker, M.P.(2017) *Why We Sleep*. London: Allen Lane.

Wallisch, P. (2008) An odd sense of timing. *Scientific American Mind*, 19(1), 37–43.

Wittgenstein, L. (1953) *Philosophical Investigations*. Oxford: Basil Blackwell.

Wittman, M. (2018) *Altered States of Consciousness: Experiences out of Time and Self*. Cambridge, MA: MIT Press.

Wolfradt, U. (2005) Strangely familiar. *Scientific American Mind*, 16(1), 32–7.

Wright, K. (2006) Times of our Lives. *Scientific American Special Edition: A Matter of Time*, 16(1), 26–33.

Wright, K. (2012) Times of our lives. *Scientific American, Special Edition*, 21(1), 34–41.

World Bank (2012) *World Development Report*. Washington, DC: World Bank.

Yalom, I.D. (2008) *Staring at the Sun: Overcoming the Dread of Death*. London: Piatkus Books.

Yarrow, K., Haggard, P., Heal, R. et al. (2001) Illusory perceptions of space and time preserve cross-saccadic perceptual continuity. *Nature*, 414, 302–5.

Zilboorg, G. (1943) Fear of Death. *Psychoanalytic Quarterly*, 12, 465–75.

Zimbardo, P. (2002) Just think about it: time to take our time. *Psychology Today*, 35, 62.

Printed in the United States
by Baker & Taylor Publisher Services